So you want to be a School Leader?

Also available from Continuum

So you want to be a Teacher? How to launch your teaching career – Lucy Waide

How to be a Successful Deputy Head – Geoff Brookes

How to be a Successful Form Tutor – Michael Marland CBE and Richard Rogers

How to be a Successful Head of Year – Brian Carline

Managing Higher Education in Colleges – Gareth Parry, Penny Blackie and Anne Thompson

Middle Management in FE – Ann Briggs

Survival Guide for College Managers and Leaders – David Collins

Ultimate FE Leadership and Management Handbook – Jill Jameson and Ian McNay

Available from Network Continuum

The Constant Leader – Max Coates

Distributing Leadership for Personalizing Learning – Ron Ritchie and Ruth Deakin Crick

Inspirations – Tim Brighouse and David Woods

Learn to Transform – David Crossley and Graham Corbyn

Personalizing Learning: How to Transform Learning Through System-Wide Reform – Phil Jones and Maureen Burns

Schools and Communities – John West-Burnham, Maggie Farrar and George Otero

Understanding Systems Leadership – Pat Collarbone and John West-Burnham

What Makes a Good School Now? – Tim Brighouse and David Woods

So you want to be a School Leader?

SHAUN MORGAN

Continuum International Publishing Group
The Tower Building   80 Maiden Lane
11 York Road   Suite 704
London SE1 7NX   New York, NY 10038

www.continuumbooks.com

British Library Cataloguing-in-Publication Data
A catalogue record for this book is available from the British Library.

ISBN: 978-1-84706-022-8 (paperback)

Library of Congress Cataloging-in-Publication Data
Morgan, Shaun.

So you want to be a school leader?/Shaun Morgan.

   p. cm. – (So you want to be?)
Includes bibliographical references.
ISBN 978-1-84706-022-8
1. School principals – Vocational guidance – Great Britain. 2. School
   management and organization – Great Britain. 3. Educational
   leadership – Great Britain. I. Title. II. Series.

LB2831.926.G7M67 2008
371.2--dc22   2008034705

Typeset by Newgen Imaging Systems Pvt Ltd, Chennai, India
Printed and bound in Great Britain by Ashford Press

So you want to be . . .

Contents

Acknowledgements

There are several people who I would like to publicly thank for helping me steer the manuscript through to publication.

I'd like to give special thanks to Debbie Morrison, OBE and Dr Philip Goggin for their honest, insightful and timely critique of the manuscript. Numerous other people also read over the manuscript prior to publication and I owe each a debt of gratitude: Jackie Lees, Jude Slack, Philip Slack, Paul Liddle and Andrew Morrison.

My family have, of course, provided me with much support. Sarah, my wife, has had to tolerate my obsessive pursuit of the project. I admit that I've been a bit of a pain during the time it took to write; I shirked my domestic duties, I complained about the pressure and I disappeared from sight for days at a time. I've also been rude to my wider family and our friends – I hope you all forgive me my transgressions.

I also must thank my mother and father, Linda and Stewart Wood – thank you for raising me to be the reasonably well-adjusted individual I am today. And I must say thank you to Mrs J for helping me unlock a little of my academic potential all those years ago.

It is only right and proper, of course, to acknowledge the countless thousands of people, and the myriad of associated interactions, both positive and negative, that have occurred over the course of my career. I have not, obviously, written anything with specific individuals in mind. But the sum of those countless interactions has created the context within which this book is set. Similarly, I owe a debt of gratitude to the academics and practitioners whose diligent work has created the theoretical backbone of this book.

Finally, then, I would like to thank Continuum for commissioning the book and therefore offering me an opportunity to scare myself a little!

Preface

Have you ever had one of those moments when you set yourself a major challenge on the spur of the moment, and then have to see it through because you don't want to lose face? Yes, well, a year or so on from that moment (a dreary afternoon in March 2007), I'm adding the final touches to this book!

My role as author, then, has been simply to create an aspirational narrative which provides practical advice and guidance for those of you who aspire to senior school leadership roles. Throughout the process of writing this book I've reflected upon and revisited those things which have proven themselves useful to me as I've developed my own leadership capabilities. I'm not suggesting that I have it all worked out, but you may find the guidance helpful.

Of course, you may not agree with some of the recommendations and you might not like the methodology. Well, just like a buffet meal, you haven't got to eat everything – so take a bit of what appeals and don't worry unduly about the rest. But I am certain that there's something for everyone. I hope the result is a no-nonsense approach to school leadership which, though far from perfect, provides a suitable starting point from which you can begin, or even accelerate, your own leadership journey.

However, in my quest to 'funk' things up a little, I offer some challenging questions, to which I do not necessarily have any answers. There are also occasions when I invite you to challenge convention, to think the unthinkable. Of course, this isn't done recklessly, but the process can be uncomfortable – see, you're intrigued now, aren't you?

Now, it is important to note that the theory contained within this book belongs to some pretty smart people. I have tried, with all sincerity, to present accurately the ideas of others as they originally intended – any failure to meet this standard is mine alone. And even if all is entirely accurate, I have not done justice to the work of these distinguished academics and practitioners, and I would therefore recommend that you read the key source material for yourself.

So, make of this book what you will. I sincerely hope that you enjoy reading this book as much as I've enjoyed writing it. I would, incidentally, welcome your feedback via the email address below. But enough of the waffle, let's get under way!

Shaun T. Morgan
shaunTmorgan@googlemail.com

1 | What's It All About?

We live in a time of unprecedented change: the knowledge economy is born and the industrial giants of old are but shadows of their former selves. And for the very first time growing numbers of people, young and old alike, have a real choice about how to live their lives. There are, however, significant challenges to face. Society is, for example, totally unprepared for the shift to personal responsibility, self-management and the execution of choice.[1] And our schooling system is still geared to telling students en masse what to do and when, which is totally inappropriate for life in the wider world at the dawn of the 21st century.[2]

Nevertheless, our education system, our schools, are at the heart of our civilization supporting the very fabric of society. And what amazing and complex organizations they are; microcosms of the communities they serve, with all the professional joy and daily trials and tribulations that come with them. To contribute to the leadership of such an organization would indeed be an honour and a pleasure, but also a significant responsibility and an awesome challenge.

Perhaps you have worked in a school for a couple of years and see yourself as a future leader. Perhaps you are to school leadership what Jean-Luc Picard is to *Star Trek* – The Next Generation!

But the everyday reality of holding a whole-school responsibility, never mind a senior leadership role, seems impossibly distant and sickeningly daunting. You are, however, passionate about education and impatient for change. You have the potential but need both reassurance and orientation.

Well, the aim is to meet both these needs. As a bare minimum, this book will identify and articulate the core attributes and competencies required of a senior school leader. If we do a good job together, perhaps you'll become convinced that a senior leadership role isn't just a fanciful dream that serves to amuse on a warm sunny day with a glass of sangria in hand. No. If we get it right, we'll see school leadership as a tangible objective to be pursued with some vigour. We may even see a map, showing the way to senior leadership, emerge before us.

Now, it's important to realize that this book will not necessarily help you to become a better classroom practitioner – this is not a book about learning and teaching per se. For the purposes of this book school leadership and classroom practice (i.e. learning and teaching) will be treated as two distinct, albeit linked, competencies. That might seem a little odd, but the key skills that make you an effective teacher, if indeed you are a teacher, will not necessarily make you an effective school manager or leader. The emphasis, then, is on the form and function of the organization and not the direct, specific, pedagogy of children. Now, you might find this view of a school somewhat disorientating – after all, you have probably spent your career putting the needs of your pupils at the very centre of your everyday practice. Of course, you can't separate a school from its students, and so the distinction is rather arbitrary, but as you shall hopefully see, this alternative organizational view will bring new and valuable insights to the school leadership role.

The idea, then, is to introduce you to some reconstituted leadership and management theory. The theory has been reconstituted to make it accessible, directly relevant to education and hopefully a little entertaining too. But the broad field of leadership and management theory is vast, and guess what, there's no one right way to go about managing a business, running a hospital or indeed leading a school; no universal laws to simply learn and apply. There are, however, common patterns of leadership behaviour, and key skills and competencies, that emerge in high-performing leaders and dynamic organizations. We will focus on identifying these patterns and key skills, but it is important that you do not take these ideas at face value – for every convincing theory, model and argument, there are equally convincing and compelling counter-arguments. We will, for example, explore key ideas in Jim Collins's books *Built to Last* (co-authored with Jerry Porras) and *Good to Great*, but many of Collins's ideas are dismissed as delusions by Phil Rosenzweig in his book *The Halo Effect*. Ultimately, it is for you to decide whether there is merit in the advice and guidance contained within this book – you will undoubtedly need to translate what you read to fit your own circumstances, so caution is urged. This book does not, then, pretend to represent the final word on school leadership and will not presume to offer a 'ten step' guide to certain leadership glory. I'll be honest, I don't of course have all the answers – I'm not even sure that I've identified all of the pertinent questions. However, I've distilled a selection of ideas and insights that may be of some use as you seek a senior leadership role in school.

As such, you could perhaps use this book as a starting point from which to begin a wider journey of discovery. Through these pages you will be encouraged to question your prevailing mindset, to think big, to dream about the future and to believe that you're capable of great things – but fear not, you won't be lulled into a euphoric trance where magical solutions, quick fixes, short cuts and instant results abound. Instead, you'll be encouraged to see the big picture, find new energy, pursue incredibly high standards (world-class standards, indeed!), challenge the status quo, think outside-of-the-box and develop new insights into yourself and your *raison d'être*. So just like the best lessons, you'll find this book to have 'pace and challenge' to help keep you engaged; this is anything but a tepid instruction manual detailing the mechanics of running a school.

This book is, indeed, but a simple guide; so make of it what you will, and take from it what you like. Of course, the work of some of the world's foremost leadership and management thinkers has been referenced, and as an aspiring leader you would find it well worth your time and effort to read their work first hand. You might pay particular attention to: Warren Bennis, Jim Collins, Stephen Covey, W. E. Deming, Peter F. Drucker, Daniel Goleman, Charles Handy and Peter Senge – plus many others whose insights are equally profound, though not perhaps as globally prominent as those belonging to this illustrious list. Now, it is important to note that the research efforts published by the National College for School Leadership (NCSL) have also been considered when writing this book. As it happens, there is some crossover between the work of the illustrious list above and the NCSL publications, as one might expect. Both are, after all, concerned with varying aspects of the same subject matter.

To Lead, But Why?

As we begin this journey, then, you need to spend some time reflecting upon your motives and values. Why do you want to become a school leader? No really, what is driving your ambition? You may already have a lifelong dream to become a headteacher, and perhaps you see your first senior role as the next important step on that journey. But you might find that you're motivated purely by the sense of securing power; that is, by the sense of feeling significant in the eyes of others – a force not to be underestimated!

Perhaps we are over-complicating the issue. Maybe you've spent the last few years developing your skills and it now just comes down to hard cash. After all, senior roles in secondary schools usually come with attractive salaries (apologies to colleagues in the primary sector who are relatively hard done by!) – you may recall Rod Tidwell, from the film *Jerry Maguire*, and his memorable catchphrase '*Show me the money!*'? Is that what you're all about? Of course, your motivation may be purely altruistic in nature – in other words, you want to make a difference to your school community by operating from a senior leadership position, regardless of any personal benefits that might be associated to the post, after all: 'School leadership is second only to classroom teaching as an influence on pupil learning.'[3] In truth, you are probably motivated by all of these factors to varying degrees, and perhaps other issues which are deeply personal to yourself. Now, it is important to note that the central assumption of this book is that these elements – personal ambition, professional significance and community contribution – are balanced as an 'Integrity Tripod'.[4] Long-term success as a senior leader depends on growth in all areas – unbridled ambition alone, for example, will cause the 'Integrity Tripod' to wobble and eventually fall.

So what about your values then? What do you stand for – what is your core educational ideology? What should schooling be all about and what are you prepared to defend to the point of resignation? Is education fundamentally concerned with learning for its own intrinsic value – a great conversation between the generations? Is it more important that a child be happy at school, even if they don't achieve – and, conversely, is it acceptable to sacrifice happiness if the child can then get results? Should education be solely geared towards preparing young people for the world of work? And should the learning environment be very businesslike, or do you prefer to see entertainment drive the learning? What factors determine effective learning and teaching in your opinion? Do you believe that a very traditional, academic curriculum should be offered to young people? Is social and emotional development crucial to achieving high levels of educational attainment? Are students entitled to have a say in core leadership and management decisions such as staff appointments and the structure of the curriculum? If you were a headteacher, what would your school look and feel like? And if you were to take over your school right now, what would you do differently?

If this is the very first time you've contemplated such questions, consider the formulation of a response to be your very first leadership and management task. If you have strong convictions about how things should be, you might find this task relatively straightforward, but don't be surprised if you find it more of a challenge. After all, there are lots of things to consider: curriculum provision, inclusion policy and practice, school ethos and identity, specialist subjects and the like. Really think this through and be ready to articulate the end of the following statement: 'If I were the Headteacher the school would . . .'

You might think that we're getting a little ahead of ourselves – we haven't even made it to the senior management/leadership team and yet we're already talking about headship. True, and there are three reasons for doing this. Firstly, you need to establish a really strong vision of your future school so you have clarity about what you stand for and how you might behave when you reach a position of considerable influence. Secondly, it is useful to see the 'horizon beyond the horizon' – by projecting your vision further forward (to headship) than your immediate goal (a senior post), the latter seems much more attainable. The world suddenly shrinks, wouldn't you agree? Thirdly, and most importantly, you'll be challenged during the course of this book to stimulate progress, to do whatever is necessary to drive improvements, while also preserving your core values. In order to do this effectively you obviously need to have a clear understanding of your core educational beliefs. Before we proceed, however, a cautionary tale is in order.

During the course of your career you will be called upon to revisit and perhaps renegotiate your core educational values and beliefs. The 'call' will come from changes in the wider world: new technology, new research findings, economic imperatives, new initiatives and political influences, among other things. Many years ago I found myself attending an end of term staff meeting at a local primary school. That year saw two members of staff leave this small school. One was leaving for pastures new and the second was taking early retirement. I sat down, with tuna and cucumber sandwich in hand, and settled in for the farewell speeches. The first to speak, a young woman, was fairly brief; she thanked the school for supporting her and expressed regret at the need to move away with her partner. So far, so good. Then, following a glowing tribute from the Head, came the teacher taking early retirement. The core message from the speech went something like this: 'For as long as I can remember, I only ever wanted to teach. It is a profession I love, it is something that I was born to do. I am therefore greatly saddened at the way things have changed over the past few years. The testing, the bureaucracy, the curriculum, the meddling and the pressure is, I feel, wrong. I want nothing more to do with it and feel that I have no choice but to take early retirement.'

It was a sad end to a distinguished career. In many regards the teacher in question was deeply principled and exceptionally courageous. I could not help but wonder, however, if the affront to his values masked a deeper issue; an inability to adapt (as opposed to an unwillingness to adapt) to fundamental, structural reform. Either way, the tale serves as a salutary lesson; your core values and beliefs are likely to be tested in these times of change.

To get us started, we're going to look at the book's overall structure and content. Each chapter is structured around a very broad leadership and management theme, so the book is best read sequentially from beginning to end. Hopefully you'll persevere through to the end because the pace-setting approach advocated, for achieving senior leadership status, will only make complete sense once you reach the end. The last chapter serves, then, to bring the process full circle, because it reminds us that we work in education for the benefit of children and the wider community. If, therefore, you do not make it to the final chapter, the book might appear unbalanced because the emphasis is otherwise on organizational leadership and management strategies without significant reference to the communities we serve. That said, let us take a look at the chapters ahead:

◆ **What's It All About?** – the remainder of this chapter is concerned with putting into context the challenge of securing a senior leadership job. The emphasis is on identifying your place in the world, the challenge we all face from globalization, and some of the basic groundwork that needs to be done.

◆ **Find Your Niche** – here we are concerned with building psychological resilience as you begin to identify opportunities to work more strategically across the school.

◆ **Tell It Like It Is!** – the concern here is the ability to develop a crystal-clear view of what's going on within your niche activity and across the wider organization. This idea then develops into securing an unrelenting focus on core activities and key outcomes.

◆ **Deliver the Goods** – this is the bottom line for those looking to secure a senior leadership role. This chapter investigates overcoming barriers to moving the school forward.

◆ **Make Like You're the Boss** – this chapter is concerned with working with others and cultivating your senior leadership persona. Do you, for example, look the part and inspire confidence among your colleagues?

◆ **Oh Yes, Don't Forget about the Children** – the quality of school leadership and management has a profound impact upon young people. This chapter reminds us that no matter how radical the approach, it is ultimately for the benefit of children and the wider community.

To Lead, But When?

How, then, do you begin to make that transition to senior leader and how long is it going to take? In terms of the latter, you might be pleased to know that it's really down to you – progress is proportional to effort. In other words, the harder and smarter you work, the quicker the journey. In terms of the former, there are various skills that you have got to acquire. If you want to operate effectively at a senior level in a school, they are non-negotiable, and if the truth be known, they can be challenging, but they must be mastered. The longer you take to get a grip of these skills the longer it will take for you to achieve your goal – it isn't therefore simply a question of time served. In fact, age or seniority is simply no longer an accurate indicator of accomplishment or expertise.[5] The pace of change, in the wider world at least, has levelled the playing field and if you work towards the adoption of 'Level 5' leadership traits – basically a combination of personal humility and unwavering resolve – you can knock years off the journey.[6]

So, you need quite literally to re-skill yourself in preparation for a senior role in school – your classroom experience will be invaluable to you, but it won't be enough on its own. We are talking here about learning to become more effective. But it is important to note that we're talking about organizational effectiveness, that is, getting things done in the interest of the wider school and not just things that are pertinent to your own, direct, professional needs.

The bottom line, if you're to be truly effective, is that you must be prepared to challenge and adjust your attitudes, acquire new knowledge, learn new skills, reflect on your experiences and become more emotionally attuned to the people around you. And the learning won't stop once you land a senior leadership role; if anything more and faster learning will then be required – but you are equal to the challenge because you are a bright and capable person of at least average intelligence. Your ability to interact successfully with others, learn new skills and adapt to changing circumstances are the factors that ultimately define your potential as a senior leader. The development of these personal attributes is critical, because once you have reached the Senior Team you'll find that the knowledge and skills you possess 'today' will be insufficient to solve the problems of 'tomorrow', due to the pace and scale of change. If that sounds a little unnerving, take comfort from the fact that everyone else faces the same predicament.

However, the good news for those of average intelligence, or above (yes, that means you!), is that school leadership is not 'rocket science'. Basically, you devise a plan and set about delivering it to the best of your ability: strategy and execution.[7] Simple really. Perhaps not quite that simple, but it's worth reflecting, for a moment or two, on the key point that it's not rocket science. Just think about how difficult rocket science really is: throw in some aerospace engineering, mathematics, fluid dynamics, material science, avionics . . . you get the idea (thanks to Wikipedia for the free rocket science lesson!), and you begin to realize that whatever you have to do to become a school leader, it isn't going to compare to the challenges of rocket science. In other words, you are perfectly capable of leading, yes leading, a school, but sometimes the everyday pressures you experience make whole-school leadership seem daunting and more difficult than it really is. That's not to trivialize the role, however. Make no mistake, membership of a school management/leadership team (SMT/SLT) is demanding work. But no matter how challenging the job gets, it still isn't as difficult as rocket science. If, by the way, you think whole-school leadership looks easy, that's because your leadership team deliberately give you that impression or, more likely, you have a very limited view of the role because much of the job is hidden. Either way, be assured, it isn't *that* easy. Challenging, but definitely not rocket science, just about sums up the situation.

The rocket science analogy may lead you to believe that the acquisition of skills and knowledge will be sufficient to secure a senior role. And, indeed, a considerable chunk of this book is concerned with just such a process. However, there is significant evidence to suggest that the development of your emotional intelligence is far more significant than specialized knowledge. Indeed, an analysis of high-performing headteachers by management consultant company Hay Group suggests that technical skills accounted for a relatively small proportion of overall leadership performance. More significant, then, is the ability to work within a team, understand others, use your initiative and motivate yourself. We cannot therefore ignore the importance of emotional intelligence, else we risk becoming technically brilliant but socially inept. We need to be fully rounded individuals in order to lead effectively; technical capability will only get us so far down the leadership road. As such, the work of leading emotional intelligence proponent Daniel Goleman will permeate this book.

Roll up Your Sleeves!

So, from the socially shy to the work-shy. If you're a little work-shy, and are out of the door come 3:30pm, we have an issue that needs to be discussed before we go any further. This book will not help you cut corners on your leadership journey, but it will help you to compress the time scales. The idea here is to identify and develop those emotional and technical competencies required to operate as a senior leader, and it is going to require discretionary effort; effort above and beyond what is required in your 'day job'. There's just no alternative, at least not for those who want to be effective, and: 'Effectiveness is a discipline. And like every discipline, effectiveness *can* be learned and *must* be earned.'[8] True, there is an implicit, and unproven, assumption here that pretty much everyone and anyone can become a good leader; that it is entirely possible to learn to be an effective leader if you put in the effort. Some people, however, do appear to develop more quickly and seem naturally predisposed to adopting and developing their leadership capabilities.[9]

Either way, time and effort will be required if you're to realize your potential. If you're not prepared to put in that time and effort – and maybe you have a young family that takes priority – maybe you're not ready for senior school leadership at this point in your life. What about work/life balance, you may ask. Of course there needs to be a balance, but time spent working as a senior leader will be incredibly intense and has the added burden of 'responsibility'. Whole-school responsibility is of a different magnitude to that which might be experienced at the subject/departmental level. At the whole-school level the buck quite literally stops with you; there is no one to bail you out if things get tough (although that's not strictly true as members of the SLT generally support each other), and there are times when things just have to be done, regardless of the time or other competing pressures. If you feel that you cannot give the required commitment to the role, perhaps your time and energy will be better spent tending to the needs of your immediate colleagues and your learners. There's absolutely nothing wrong with saying 'actually, no, this isn't for me. I have neither the time nor the inclination to put even more effort into my job. I do more than enough already, thank you'. Fair enough, enough said.

Commit to the Process

So, can you, fundamentally, find the extra energy required to make your senior leadership dream become a reality within a relatively short period of time? Can you learn to think and act in new ways, or are you destined to become a dinosaur because one 'can't teach an old dog new tricks'? And if you can find the extra energy, you might wonder why you'd want to go through something that is clearly going to be demanding and time-intensive. Presumably you picked up this book because you want to get a move on in your career and make a difference to the community you serve. Perhaps you see a world of opportunity out there in 'education land' and only, if only, you had more influence, you could lead the agenda, do the right things, get the job done and make a big impact. Hold on to that idealism because it is for those reasons that you will 'go the extra mile' and subject yourself to challenging tasks for the apparent fun of it. And when the going gets tough, and it will, your idealism will sustain you. For the materialists out there: you'll be well rewarded. For the spiritualists: you'll be professionally fulfilled. Actually, it won't take you long to realize that the journey is the reward because the process will literally expand your mind and clarify your thinking.[10] So what's the problem with a little hard work when the potential returns are so great for both you and your school community?

As we begin our journey, then, it is necessary to start by taking a good look around yourself and to consider the challenges we face as school leaders of the future. We undoubtedly live in a time of unprecedented change; a time of initiative overload and far-reaching public sector reform. Schools are now expected to offer extended services such as childcare, parenting support, swift and easy access to specialist services and adult learning services. We also live in a time of accelerating economic globalization, a phenomenon that appears to be enriching upper and middle England and, paradoxically, highlighting both the educational underachievement of the British workforce and the plight of a significant socio-economic underclass. Our education system is, consequently, under pressure as never before and there are no signs that the pressure will ease in the near future. Large numbers of young people are leaving school and are literally dropping out of society by becoming NEET (Not in Employment, Education or Training). Officially they numbered around 206,000 in 2006[11] – but because they exist as a statistical construct, rather than a physical head count, there might be many more.

There also appears to be a literacy and numeracy crisis hitting the country. Apparently there are millions of British adults without basic skills; that is, seven million who lack functional numeracy and five million who lack functional literacy skills.[12] Consider also that approximately 50 per cent of the Army's recruits (5000–6000 annually) have literacy and numeracy skills at or below Entry 3 – that means they would struggle to achieve a grade G at GCSE.[13]

Apart from the grim waste of human potential that invariably arises when people cannot properly read, write or count, the damage to the national economy is significant. Learndirect, the UK national e-learning service for adults, reckons that 14.6 million working adults have made basic errors and lost their company money.

So, we are in a position where those becoming NEET are condemning themselves to a life of social exclusion, and a significant proportion of those going to work have barely the skills to get by, never mind help their organizations compete in the global marketplace. Can we, as a nation, continue to absorb these issues in the face of continuing global economic trends?

In all fairness, the government and schools are responding; the 14–19 agenda brings the promise of diplomas and the introduction of formal functional skills testing, and the DCSF (Department for Children, Schools and Families) is planning, at the time of writing, to raise the school leaving age to 18. So to be fair to the government, there has been increased investment and some out-of-the-box thinking over the past few years. Similarly, many schools have already revamped their curriculum and introduced vocational courses. Many have, indeed, adopted new technology to enhance personalized learning, and driven through countless other initiatives to help engage and motivate young people. So schools have responded to the challenges, but will of course continue to have a big part to play in improving standards. If that doesn't add up to a land of opportunity for the aspiring leader, what does? It will be challenging, but it won't be full-blown rocket science.

You might be interested to know, then, that over the next few years there is predicted to be a headship crisis; the present incumbents are retiring at a rate quicker than they can be replaced – and there isn't exactly a stampede to replace them! Sure, plenty of people are going through the NPQH programme (National Professional Qualification for Headship), but they appear to be unwilling to step up – only 43 per cent of NPQH graduates go on to headship after five years.[14] It would appear then, that you might have a fairly clear run at a headship if you're so inclined.

Grasp the Wider Context

Anyway, we digress. The broader point here is that schools operate within phenomenally complex national, and international, contexts and it is important to gain some understanding of the national agendas that influence educational policy, even if you think the link between a national economic issue and education is tenuous. The state of the national economy, and indeed the future needs of the economy, probably have a greater strategic influence on policy than we realize.[15] After all, what is the point of education, if not to equip and prepare young people to eventually sustain the economy upon which we all fundamentally rely? Perhaps education is intrinsically valuable as a means to its own end, but you need to become aware of the tensions that drive the agenda and to question the motives of those in power. Now, catching up on current affairs probably isn't everyone's idea of fun, but unless you regularly read a decent newspaper and engage with other sources of credible news how else will you gain a deeper insight into the national agendas?

It is perhaps tempting to think that the national agenda is far removed from your everyday professional experiences. However, the pace of reform is such that it's only a matter of time before you feel the effects. So spend a little time finding out about academies and the building schools for the future (BSF) programme. Why not also conduct a little research into trust schools, training schools, extended schools, specialist schools and foundation schools, as a starting point? The thing is, when one of these initiatives affects your school, people will be asking a lot of questions and not many people will have answers – except for you that is. And suddenly you will have an opportunity to become the in-house authority on the subject. Suddenly, you will have an informed opinion which others want to hear and, consequently, you'll have an opportunity to influence the agenda. But you might be thinking: 'That's all well and good, but if something like that doesn't happen, I'll have wasted my time researching and reading up.' Not so. Remember, we're trying to acquire the skills of a senior leader and keeping abreast of developments is part of the role. And besides, your research will lead to a more sophisticated understanding of the entire educational system, so you need to make like a Boy Scout and 'be prepared'!

Okay, you've got your head around some of the national agendas, but we're not done yet. The wonderful mysteries that are the local authority are waiting to be unravelled. Senior school leaders work with their local authorities on a wide range of agendas; there's behaviour and attendance data to collect, personnel and school finance to manage, admissions and transition to arrange, school performance and attainment data to analyse – plus a whole load of other things that need to be sorted out. Chances are, you have met LA subject advisors but are 'out of the loop' on many of the other agendas because you don't need to worry about them. As a staff member at the operational end of the organization (i.e. a classroom teacher or non-teacher going about your daily business) you're quite happy with this state of affairs because you're free to concentrate on your job. As an aspiring leader, however, you can't afford to live in blissful ignorance because people are making decisions and the process is a mystery to you – those people who comprise the senior leadership team obviously know what's going on and it's now your job to find out more. The first thing to do is try to get your head around the structure of the local authority. Who has the influence? What is the link between the council chief executive and the Director of Children's Services? What is the organizational structure in terms of roles and responsibilities? Who are the local councillors? It will probably take you some time to fully answer these kind of questions, particularly if you work in a large local authority. And the significance of some people and their roles will be lost on you until you have cause to interact with them.

You might be wondering about the point of this exercise. Well, it's very simple really – you will eventually get to meet these people and by knowing their names and roles you'll be able to quickly establish rapport and discuss things going on across the school or authority. Similarly, when you chat to members of the leadership team about whole-school business, and they name drop, you won't be staring back with a blank expression on your face! We're talking about your first steps into networking at both the senior level in school and at local authority level.

Having an understanding about how the local authority works is one thing, but you will also find that there are dozens of other organizations that impact locally on a school. One of the purposes of the Every Child Matters (ECM) legislation is to strengthen the multi-agency partnerships that support vulnerable children and their families. There should be, as a consequence, closer integration between education, social services, police, health, non-governmental organizations (possibly charities and housing associations) and many others, that deliver support services. You need to develop your understanding of these structures, even if they don't immediately and obviously impact on your daily practice – a good place to start is the ECM website.[16]

There is one further mysterious group that is influential in school, though typically removed from your everyday experiences. Yes, the governors. The role of the governing body ranges from appointing the headteacher to setting, in partnership with senior staff, the strategic direction of the school – all key decisions about the school are made via the governors. There is no need to go into great detail about the structure and function of the governors because there is a great website which explains it all, and is well worth visiting.[17] The key point about the governing body, however, is that there are designated places for teaching and support staff from the school. If you want to get noticed by the leadership team, and want to take a big step towards securing a leadership role, why not talk to your headteacher, or other senior staff, about securing a position on the governing body? You'll be asked to attend termly evening meetings, at the very least, and you'll be asked to sit on various subcommittees that deal with things like personnel, finance and curriculum. But you're not concerned about the extra work or time commitment, are you? Of course not. You might have to be patient because there may not be an immediate vacancy. And when a vacancy does arise, you may have to face fellow colleagues in a vote to secure the place.

Now, you may have been working in a school for a few years, clocking up the hours in the classroom or working away in a support staff role. You might, alternatively, be fairly new and mega-ambitious! If therefore the organizational structure is a bit of a mystery and you don't know who holds the key responsibilities, have a read of the school handbook or ask a senior member of staff to explain the structure. You might also be interested to know that NCSL offer, at the time of writing, a fast-track leadership programme for those in the early years of their teaching career[18] – so you must be a qualified teacher to join the programme.

It should be clear that if you're to become a senior school leader you need to keep your wits about you, learn new skills and become politically astute. It is easy to get locked into your daily routine and subsequently lock out other things that are going on around you. If you're prone to this, and we all are to a certain extent, you must resolve to lift up your head, so to speak, and take a good look around at what's going on. But, in fact, more than this is required because, although passive observation will help you to fill gaps in your knowledge, learning will best take place when you proactively engage with the activity going on around you – this means going out to ask questions, finding things to read and getting involved. The proactive approach will better protect you from a 'Who is Ed Balls?'

moment – those moments when you ask a question that clearly shows you're a bit wet behind the ears, a bit non compos mentis, and which can provide much mirth and amusement for your colleagues!

See the Big Picture

You are, then, mapping out for yourself the organizational and political landscape. You are looking to see where you, and your colleagues, fit in the bigger picture. This process is vitally important because you will begin to differentiate the operational domain from the strategic domain of the organization.

Equally important is your new resolve to shine the light of curiosity onto the those dark corners of ignorance that exist for you in your school like, for example, the names and roles of those mysterious LA people. This isn't an academic exercise though. The ability to look out across 'education land' is an essential senior leadership skill – great leaders grasp the broad context within which they work and can, consequently, spot opportunities and avoid potential pitfalls.[19] And once you have secured your SLT role, you'll find that you continue to scan the landscape, but the scale will be different; you might instead look out at provision mapped across school clusters, or local authorities, or even the entire country! The ability to sweep a proverbial searchlight across the landscape is but half of the story, however. When appropriate you'll need to use laser-like vision to drill down into a topic or an issue affecting the school.[20]

So, things have to be very different from now on. You now need to see yourself and your school very differently. You are not a drone blindly following routine with concern only for your own patch, your own students and your own subjects. This is an important shift to make in your thinking and outlook because individuals who are only concerned with their specific role have little sense of responsibility for the organiza-tion's overall performance.[21] So, you want a say in wider school matters and are now concerned with the quality of provision in other areas. Are pupils getting a fair deal in subject x? Is learn-ing and teaching at least satisfactory? Are resources effectively used? Is leadership and management good? Is overall school performance acceptable? A word of warning though. You are absolutely not going to suddenly start charging around the place offering your forthright opinions about the quality of other people's work – not a good way to win friends and influ-ence people! So when you're looking at other aspects of the school's performance bear the following Chinese proverb in mind: 'He who treads softly goes far.'

In fact, it would be wise not to say anything to anyone at school, at least not for now, about your leadership ambitions. What is required at this point is sustained curiosity while you're checking things out. If you like to have things out in the open and think that keeping quiet about your leadership ambition is a little Machiavellian, you should think again. You see, if you start making grand declarations, you will put your-self under unnecessary pressure and people will be watch-ing for a future stumble or fall – do you really need that kind of pressure? Perhaps not, so keep it to yourself. And besides this, you may spend several months doing the preparatory work described above and decide that, actually, senior leader-ship isn't your thing after all. If you have your ambition under wraps until you're certain of your future direction, you won't feel as though you have to back-track.

No QTS? No Problem!

The idea of striking out for senior leadership is challenging for anyone, but if you happen to be a member of support staff in a school it is all the more daunting. Recent workforce remodelling has led to a dramatic diversification of roles in school for those who do not hold qualified teacher status (QTS) – assuming that your school has enthusiastically embraced the initiative.[22] Can, therefore, a member of support staff ever hope to join the senior team? Well, many already have, though their roles tend to be limited to personnel, business development, finance and premises, although this is changing as the boundaries are pushed. If you work in a school and do not hold QTS, do not assume this to be an automatic barrier to senior leadership – true, your journey will be more problematic because there are no clearly defined career routes to senior leadership for support staff, but the journey is not impossible. To paraphrase Hannibal: you must either find a way, or make one. So, you will 'plough your own furrow', so to speak, but if you're determined enough, and are prepared to put in the required effort, you will succeed.

However, you'll have to learn to reject 'no' as a final answer. You'll have to challenge rules, regulations and pay structures. You may have to challenge entrenched assumptions about the 'place' of support staff in schools and you'll have to live with discomfort. But you're equal to the challenge. You might take some comfort from a recently published review of school leadership by a company called PricewaterhouseCoopers (PwC).[23] One of the key messages is that the nature of school leadership is becoming more diverse, more complex, and that traditional 'Hero Head' approaches are no longer adequate. So, school leadership needs to become more distributed and there is room, in education land, for a non-teaching chief operating officer to replace the headteacher role. After all, is it realistic to assume that no one else in the country is well equipped to lead and manage a school other than those who hold QTS? Now you might have some strong opinions about that, but as far as we're concerned here, we're all equal in our pursuit of senior leadership. What we individually bring to the table in terms of leading a school is somewhat incidental because, as we discussed earlier, classroom practice (i.e. learning and teaching) and school leadership and management are two discrete, albeit linked, competencies.

Perhaps, as someone with QTS, you're disturbed by the thought of non-teaching specialists turning up to lead the senior team? Well, keep an open mind and consider the potential benefits that other leadership models might bring to our quest for world-class standards. There's a little bit of 'devil's advocate' going on here, but it is likely that a non-QTS person will lead a school or an academy in the not too distant future – not least because a small number of people without QTS are successfully completing NPQH. So, we're all friends and close colleagues here. We're all passionate and motivated individuals in pursuit of excellence for both our children and the wider school community.

So, what is it all about? It is definitely about meeting the challenge to secure world-class standards in education, because globalization demands nothing less – it is reasonable to assume that life in the mid to latter half of the 21st century is going to be pretty grim for those of us, children and adults alike, who cannot, or will not, respond to the challenges posed by emerging economies like China and India. To paraphrase author Stephen Covey, it's now time for many individuals and organizations to make a quantum leap in performance, else it's business as usual, and that simply isn't good enough anymore.[24] It is also about looking at school leadership differently, by building upon best practice within the education sector, but also by assimilating best practice from the wider business world.

Finally then, it is about you, the next generation of school leader. Can you find the energy and passion to pursue senior leadership? Can you embrace the idea that you are your own best teacher and can therefore learn anything you put your mind to?[25] And can you learn to nurture an organization as you might a child – sometimes with tenderness, and sometimes with 'tough love'? So, with open mind, a big heart and steely determination, your journey to senior leadership gets under way. Read on!

2 | Find Your Niche

'Destiny is not a matter of chance, it is a matter of choice; it is not a thing to be waited for, it is a thing to be achieved.'

William Jennings Bryan

As paradoxical as it may sound, the journey to senior school leadership isn't primarily concerned with mastering the mechanics of running a school. Before it will be possible to get a grip of the rules, regulations, systems and structures that make a school tick, it is necessary to embark upon a journey of *personal mastery* – that is, a voyage towards self-understanding, control and improvement.

You can easily identify those who are already engaged with this process; they seem to have a special sense of purpose driving their vision and shaping their values and they see change as an ally, not an assailant. Such people are deeply inquisitive about the world around and want to gaze upon reality without rose-tinted spectacles. If such individuals appear calm and collected it is because they are at peace with themselves and feel connected to those around.[1] Such people do not feel compelled to justify their existence or boast about their achievements. They do not descend to petty bickering or telling tales. And they do not denigrate the accomplishments of their friends, family or colleagues. Instead they seek to further their learning; to build upon their strengths and minimize their weaknesses. They seek, ultimately, to secure profound meaning in both their personal and professional lives.

In order to realize profound personal change, so argue Senge and his colleagues, a deep and holistic view of the world is required. Essentially, it goes like this. Cultivate a vivid awareness of 'now'. Then work to develop a deep understanding of both yourself and your interconnectedness with the wider world and, finally, learn to act in new ways which have a positive impact on the 'whole'. The process can be distilled into a very simple model: thinking, learning, doing.[2] However, the key characteristics are the depth of the self-awareness and the impact of subsequent actions.

A Personal Vision

To begin your own journey towards personal mastery, you might construct a vision – an image of your future self, making sure to contemplate both your personal circumstances and your professional role. Time spent cultivating this vision will be well spent because the process will help you to refine your core values and beliefs and develop your self-confidence.

You will begin to gain a better understanding of your 'purpose' in life – a purpose that goes beyond meeting your immediate needs: paying the mortgage, the gas bill and the like. You will see the importance of taking steps which lead to a higher goal, rather than simply perpetuating a routine whose measure of success might involve limping, exhausted, to the next holiday period. Of course, holidays are important to recharge the batteries, but they obviously aren't a means to their own end. Your journey towards personal mastery inevitably involves thinking through the contribution you intend to make to civilization while you have the chance. Now is the time to shape the world around you.

And so there isn't a breed of superhuman who has the exclusive right to shape society, though they undoubtedly existed in the formal class systems and industrial models of old. No, you are as equally entitled as anyone else to step forward and exert an influence, to shape the future. It does, however, take confidence to exercise the right to express an opinion. You also need to be resilient and humble in order to handle the feedback, which can sometimes be harsh, and which inevitably comes when expressing your opinions in a democratic society.

Anyway, it's important to take this process of personal mastery seriously because whatever you aim to achieve in life, know that success requires, first and foremost, an act of imagination.[3] You have to know what the end-game looks like so that you can have a clear idea of both the destination and your current position. We might therefore 'begin with the end in mind'.[4]

Self-belief is Everything

Now, two deeply ingrained beliefs tend to underpin our everyday behaviour and therefore affect our ability to create the future we really desire: powerlessness and unworthiness.[5] In life, we have commitments to meet and expectations to fulfil and are consequently left with little capacity to accomplish important goals and therefore realize our dreams. It is, however, necessary to question the value of these other commitments – are they really so important that they take precedence over activities that would bring your desired future into being?

Let's just reflect for a moment on this point – we're talking about choosing actions which either move you closer to your ambitions and dreams and activities that, for whatever reason, do not make a contribution to that journey. And, although this book is concerned with moving your career forward, this point applies equally to any aspect of your life that could be better: diet and exercise, relationships with family, colleagues, friends, and so on. How much attention are you giving to the really important things in life? Stephen Covey suggests that you contemplate the day you are finally laid to rest and ask whether, in the final reckoning, you are likely to be pleased with yourself, or whether you will feel that you've sold yourself short.

So just because you are very busy does not necessarily mean that you are effective at moving life forward in a desirable direction. Look, if you really are so busy that you just can't make the important things happen: healthy eating, taking more exercise, visiting relatives/friends, starting a course, taking on additional responsibilities and the like, that's fine. But the shocking truth is that it's only a belief that you can't accomplish these goals.

What you need, as an antidote to feelings of powerlessness, is a dose of self-efficacy – a belief in your own ability to perform a task and achieve a goal. The possession of self-efficacy is a key leadership and management characteristic because it determines how long you will persist in the face of failure or difficulty. The stronger your self-efficacy the longer you'll endure.[6] This is such an important trait because your fabulous future will not come to pass without a struggle. If your journey to senior leadership turns into a proverbial quagmire, you must not give up: 'If you are going through hell, keep going', Winston Churchill once advised. Actually, it is during a time of crisis, a period of self-doubt with impossible demands and insufficient time, that your leadership mettle will form. During such moments you will either grow and achieve new levels of personal mastery, or else become jaded and damaged by the experience.[7] I'm always reminded of the phrase 'Cometh the hour, cometh the man', muttered by cricketer Cliff Gladwin during a brutal encounter with South African bowlers. You see, when things get tough, those with the highest levels of self-efficacy ultimately overcome their powerless belief system and go on to achieve outstanding results, whereas the rest give up and go home.

You will therefore begin to discover your 'place' in the world, the limit of your capabilities. But this limit is just an illusion – you can make further progress in your career, but you may opt out because you perceive the price of progress to be too high – whether the cost be emotional turmoil, time or effort. Nevertheless, your limitations essentially stem from the choices you make, though your powerless belief system insists that external factors are to blame. There's a lot at stake for those who recognize their potential and yet feel powerless before the world. If you should give up because you believe the journey to be too difficult, you may find yourself embroiled in a different kind of emotional turmoil: 'Depression is the emotion that comes in the wake of helplessness, individual failure and unrealized attempts to gain power.'[8]

We're Not Worthy!

Even if, however, you believe that you do have the power to achieve your goals, you may hold the belief that you're not good enough to become a school leader and don't deserve to be happy and successful. How unfortunate would it be if the most significant barrier to your career progression was an insidious belief that you are unworthy? As we've already seen, there are no superhumans holding an entitlement, an absolute right, to lead others. You are just as worthy a candidate for leadership as any other individual. The only thing that differentiates you from others is your effectiveness in the role, and effectiveness is a capability which must be both earnt and learnt by everyone. If the politicians are to be believed, we live in a true meritocracy – those who can demonstrate their effectiveness will have an opportunity to make progress.

So, it is important to reflect on your life so far, to look forward to your future and recognize that you, and not external factors, have personal responsibility for 'you'. As such, you can only reflect upon your early life in the hope of understanding it. But your destiny is your own and you can do everything about the rest of your life and your career.[9] These strong psychological forces must be tamed before you can make the required conceptual leap to aspiring senior leader, and it is necessary to renegotiate and reconstruct your personal beliefs about the way the world works, how you subsequently respond and where you believe you belong.[10]

Mental Models

And it turns out that we have 'mental models' of the world which, in turn, direct our behaviour. These models are programs installed into us by our life experiences.[11] This programming creates our beliefs, which in turn gives rise to our attitudes, and our attitudes are at the root of our feelings. Our feelings determine our actions and, yes, actions create results.[12] Changing our behaviour to get better results therefore depends upon us changing our programming, but this is incredibly difficult because our attitudes, feelings and beliefs get in the way. This is why our early life experiences are so vitally important to realizing our future potential and why affecting a culture change in our organizations is so challenging. We might *know* in our mind that we need to change, but also not *feel* like changing.

We are not, however, destined always to respond in our old pre-programmed ways – we can indeed rewrite the program, but we have to unpick those deeply held assumptions so as to identify and eventually eradicate obsolete and unhelpful ways of thinking, and their corresponding behaviours. As a result of this process we can then adopt new modes of behaviour appropriate to the senior leadership role.[13]

As it happens, the whole idea that we can change ourselves, that we as individuals have control over our own destiny, has slowly dawned on mankind over the centuries, culminating, indeed, in the many facets of the self-improvement industry we see today. We are ultimately seeking 'self-actualization' – to *be* all that we *can*, which sits at the zenith of Maslow's famous hierarchy of needs.[14] Once there, we will experience the world without prejudice, we will become deeply inquisitive about the nature of our conscious experiences and will, indeed, find creative solutions to seemingly intractable problems. It sounds like a great psychological place to occupy, which is why the journey to senior leadership is the real reward, rather than extraneous artefacts such as a job title and salary. It is, perhaps, only in retrospect that the full gravity of this realization comes to bear.

We will therefore assume that our character is not fixed; that we have the innate ability to improve ourselves, though you should know that the counter-argument insists that it's all down to biology. Nevertheless, we will stick to the premise that we are conditioned by our life experiences, and that we now need to gain conscious control of ourselves and learn to recondition our thinking in order to change our behaviour and get better results.

Conditioning the Mind

Now, the idea of mental conditioning might start alarm bells ringing; after all, the very thought of it conjures up images of despotic regimes brainwashing the masses into doing their evil bidding. However, consider for a moment, if you will, physical conditioning, in comparison to this kind of psychological conditioning.

If we decided to go out and run a marathon, most of us would require a considerable amount of physical training, not to say some very significant incentives! If we had the inclination, imagination, dedicated time and an appropriate training regime, most people would be successful at completing the challenge. However, the thought of trying to run a marathon without doing the preparation is, quite frankly, mad, and no one would seriously expect you to be successful. And that is the key point – it is impossible to achieve the goal without considerable, intensive preparation.

Is it therefore realistic to expect to become an effective leader without first preparing yourself, psychologically speaking, for the role? Granted, the marathon analogy doesn't accurately reflect the challenges of leadership – not least because a marathon is a one-off event and leadership is an ongoing role. But school leadership is challenging; and the ability to get results, learn new skills and to adapt to change will require, among other things, enhanced psychological resilience. Notice, then, the issue here is about your attitudes and not necessarily your skills and knowledge. If you are to be successful you need to challenge and change your attitude, because, as we have already seen, a better attitude ultimately leads to better results. That doesn't mean, however, that you necessarily have a 'bad' attitude, it's just that you need to evolve your patterns of thinking and behaviour in order to create the psychological capacity to take your professional practice and career to the next level.

But this kind of preparation, this reprogramming, must be absolutely aligned with our core values. We must not submit to any activity which is not in harmony with the correct principles.[15] Nor must such activity be imposed upon an individual by an organization, as management expert Peter Drucker points out: 'To use psychology to control, dominate, and manipulate others is self-destructive abuse of knowledge. It is also a repugnant form of tyranny.'[16] So, the decision to embark upon a journey of personal mastery, with its associated cognitive reconditioning, has to be taken voluntarily and aligned with your core values, thereby inoculating you against any attempt by a despotic regime – government or corporate – from hijacking your mind for their evil purposes! Ultimately it is an undertaking that you cannot be forced or cajoled into beginning.

So, if you have developed, following the earlier exercise, a clear vision of your future professional life, seek now to add the detail. Imagine, if you will, that you have achieved your goal of securing a job with the senior leadership team. In your mind's eye look to see what you are doing in that post. Are you leading meetings with parents and students? Are you delivering training on the latest government initiative to your colleagues? Are you representing the school at a national conference? Are you meeting with the rest of the senior team? People who operate at the top of their chosen profession visualize themselves in role, performing various tasks. Use this technique to create a vivid sensation of your future professional life; feel it, see it, before you actually come to live it.[17] As I write this section, I have a very clear vision of this book sitting on the shelf of a high-street bookshop. I can 'see' the cover, even though it hasn't yet been designed. I can 'hear' words of both praise and scorn from you, the audience, even though they have yet to be spoken. And I'm aware of how I feel about publishing my first book; which tends to range from unbridled excitement to overwhelming fear. This vision, feelings included, drives me to complete the project to the best of my ability, regardless of other issues currently competing for my time.

When you engage in this visualization activity, for your senior leadership journey, you might perhaps think that the vision of your future self is but a flight of fancy. It's not real, you can't make it real, so let's get it packed into a little box and forget about it. We know, don't we, that this kind of thinking is rooted in either the powerlessness or unworthiness belief system. So let's learn to deal with it.

The Power of Self-talk

To start with, it is very important to get a grip of what might be described as your self-talk – that little voice which provides a running commentary in your head. Positive self-talk can be hugely beneficial by promoting self-belief. No, actually that's an understatement of gargantuan proportions. The application of positive self-talk is responsible for the difference between those who live an insubstantial and unfulfilled life and those who shine in their chosen endeavours. Unsurprisingly, negative self-talk can be shockingly debilitating. Now, it seems reasonable to assume that if you're saying to yourself 'I can't do this . . . I'm not good enough . . . People will laugh at me . . . What am I doing here . . . I haven't got enough experience . . .', and so on, you are going to be talking yourself out of doing things that you're actually perfectly capable of doing. And the fact that you have this narrative running around your head is evidence of how deeply ingrained into your psyche these beliefs actually are. Old habits die hard and it will be no mean feat to overcome a pre-programmed response associated to a particular task or event. How many times, for example, has something happened and your self-talk and self-speak (comments said out loud) run away in the excitement of the moment? You're in a meeting and knock a glass of water over and say out loud; 'Sorry! I'm so clumsy!' and internally the dialogue continues as you mop up; 'I'm such a bloody clumsy idiot when I'm at these meetings – what the hell is wrong with me?' Sound familiar?

Well, use self-talk instead to say positive things to yourself, because: 'Changing the destructive things you say to yourself when you experience the setbacks that life deals all of us is the central skill of optimism.'[18] So when the next setback occurs, try saying this instead: *'Right now, today, this very moment, I am capable of giving myself the gift of absolute self-assurance, self-belief, and powerful non-stop confidence in myself.'*[19] These positive self-talk statements are also known as affirmations. If you struggle to control your self-talk, try using affirmations as a tool to recondition your mental model. Affirmations can be recorded and replayed, or they can be written and read back. They are usually presented in the first person and in the present tense; 'I am', 'I can', as opposed to the future tense, for example, 'I will'. Some further examples, then, courtesy of Dr Shad Helmstetter, author of *What to Say When You Talk to Yourself*:[20]

◆ I do only those things which are best for me. I create the best within myself, I attract the best in others, and I find the best in the world around me.

◆ I allow no one else, at any time, to assume control or responsibility over my life or over anything that I do. My responsibility to others is an extension of my own responsibility to myself.

◆ I am intelligent. My mind is quick and alert and clever and fun. I think good thoughts, and my mind makes things work right for me.

◆ I do not fear problems, I solve them. I do not ignore problems, I confront them. I do not avoid problems, I conquer them.

◆ I keep my mind too busy thinking good, healthy, positive, constructive and productive thoughts to ever have any time for worry.

We can also use self-talk to make unpleasant tasks a little more bearable. Helmstetter tells a story about a friend's aunt who loathes cooking but does it in order to care for her family properly. As she goes off to the kitchen, however, she would say to herself, 'This is going to be fun. I'm going to have a good time cooking today.'[21]

If you're reading this with a degree of scepticism and would prefer instead to continue saying negative and unhelpful things to yourself, in order to reaffirm your current mental model of the world, well, that's up to you. If you have an alternative strategy that deals with the problem, that's great. If, however, you are sceptical, yet do want to change, set your doubt to one side and instead engage with this process: Write down three affirm-ations and repeat them to yourself at least five times every morning and evening for two weeks and see if you notice a difference. Now, you might start to notice a change, but get this – the self-talk messages need constant reinforcement. You will not affect a permanent change in the quality of your self-talk unless you are obsessively committed to the process.[22] Positive self-talk is a habit of mind which cannot be induced through a quick fix.

Getting a grip of your self-talk in order to change you mental models is critical to your future success. You will other-wise be in conflict when the time comes to step up to the next level of your professional development. Ultimately, you have to develop an optimistic 'can-do' attitude running to your core if you are to make progress in your career, never mind hasten your journey to the senior team. Of course, you can't simply talk yourself into believing you're good enough – that would be somewhat naive. But you can be absolutely certain that, regardless of whatever else is required for a leadership role, a high level of self-belief is a key ingredient for long-term suc-cess. As the well-worn quote, attributed to Henry Ford, goes: 'Whether you believe you can or believe you can't, you're prob-ably right.'

Beware the Comfort Zone

During your senior leadership journey there will undoubt-edly come times of self-doubt and deep discomfort – well, no one said this process was going to be easy! Now, your improved self-talk will help you to deal with discomfort, but beware the temptation to retreat when things start to get really tough. Perhaps you are familiar with the idea of comfort zones – lovely psychological spaces where we are safe and cozy, where our knowledge is secure, our remit and boundaries clear, and where we are protected from the nasty challenges of everyday working life. We probably need comfort zones in order to preserve our sanity and function on a day-to-day basis, but it can be argued that comfort zones are potential 'tar pits' that bog us down and keep us from realizing our full potential.

When you begin to have an input into areas of the school other than those that you have traditionally considered to be your own, you begin to step outside your comfort zone – 'What gives me the right?' might be a typical self-talk comment you make to yourself. You might begin to worry about the reaction of colleagues to your supposed intrusion, and that worry might stop you from asking perfectly legitimate questions, or taking perfectly legitimate action – after all, it's best not to upset people. So stay in 'your' area of the school, regardless of whatever authority might have been delegated to you by the headteacher, and those unpleasant feelings will go away. Next thing you know, you'll have talked yourself out of doing the things necessary to move yourself and the school forward. Okay, let's be blunt about this one: get over it. The longer it takes you to adjust to conducting yourself in a broader and more senior capacity, the longer your journey to the senior team.

Now there are various means through which you may come to make a wider contribution to the organization, which we'll discuss shortly, but procrastination due to discomfort is likely to lead to missed opportunities. Imagine how many missed opportunities you might accumulate over the next twenty years if you don't learn to break out of your comfort zone. Think back and consider how many opportunities you've already missed for this same reason. As Mark Twain points out: 'Twenty years from now you will be more disappointed by the things that you didn't do than by the ones you did do . . .'

It's obviously very important to break this cycle because fear, or unworthiness, or powerlessness, or hesitation or whatever you want to call it, will sometimes be the only thing that's holding you back, and it will crop up time and again during your leadership journey. The unfortunate truth is that when you take charge of your own destiny, it can be both uncomfortable and unpopular at times, but staying in your comfort zone will do little to stimulate progress.[23] You might be interested to know that I too am painfully aware of my own 'unworthiness' when it comes to writing a book of this nature, but I'll do it anyway because I cannot allow the opportunity to pass. Personal growth is indeed uncomfortable.

So it is important that you both recognize the comfort zone for what it potentially is, a 'tar pit', and learn to deal with it, difficult though it sometimes is. You might be pleased to know, however, that once the internal picture of yourself finally adjusts, and your new, more senior persona emerges, any discomfort you initially felt will disappear – in other words you will have extended your comfort zone. And by that time you'll be ready to 'see' yourself as a deputy headteacher or a headteacher, and so the cycle will begin again.

Okay, admittedly there's a bit of 'pop psychology' going on here and perhaps such significant aspects of the human condition cannot be readily distilled into a few basic concepts that would probably struggle to stand up to scientific scrutiny. It is worth pointing out that the management expert Peter Drucker was having none of it: 'Contrary to everything that modern psychologists tell you, I am convinced that one can acquire knowledge, one can acquire skills, but one cannot change his personality.'[24] Nevertheless, psychological toughness, optimism and self-belief, however you manage to acquire them, are required. And if you haven't currently 'got it', and believe that you can't change your personality, you've got a problem. I guess it comes down to a choice: give up or go onwards.

Here's your chance to disprove Drucker. Continue the senior leadership journey, overcome your programmed limitations, and choose to fulfil your potential.

Making a Contribution

So what mechanism can you use to make a contribution to other aspects of the school – it is, after all, rather rude just to walk around and make random comments to your colleagues about how to improve things. Now, if we consider your current relationship with the organization as a straightforward transaction, you might ask: 'What do I have that you want, and what do I get in return?' You already offer the school a service of some kind because you're an employee, and you obviously get paid in exchange for your services. If you're in the classroom teaching children for 95 per cent of the time, your role is fundamentally operational and therefore limited, in terms of leading and managing the wider organization. Learning and teaching are obviously at the core of the organization, that's the whole point of a school, but this book isn't about being an effective teacher; it is about being an effective leader and manager. And if you are to become an effective leader and manager, you have to perform tasks that have an impact across the wider school. And that basically means you need to 'break out' of your classroom, or your comparative non-teaching role. So, you now need to offer something more, something that marks you out as an aspiring leader with potential to join the senior leadership team. This shift in outlook is going to require self-belief and a definite departure from the comfort zone.

So, what additional contribution can you make? This is not a question to answer in haste. If, ultimately, you're to have an impact at a senior level you'll need to develop a distinctive set of skills and you'll need to think carefully about your professional interests. You might therefore start by asking yourself a question: 'What can I contribute that will significantly affect the performance and results of the institution I serve?'[25] Let us get something immediately and absolutely clear, as it will set the tone for the rest of the book. This is not simply a question about any random contribution to the wider organization. Absolutely not. You might contribute, for example, by agreeing to supervise students on trips out. You might, indeed, offer to organize important events like parents' evenings and the like. These are valuable contributions in their own right, and they will certainly keep you busy, and will be very much appreciated by your colleagues. However, these activities are not likely, in and of themselves, *to significantly affect the performance and results* of the institution you serve. This is a very important point.

As an aspiring senior leader, you might like to consider contributing to activities that have an impact on the performance and results of those things which your organization values most highly. If your school values drama, boys' achievement, computing or languages, for example, think about how you might contribute to those areas. A focus in such key areas is very important for two reasons. Firstly, you are demonstrating 'alignment' with the school's vision and ethos – that is, pulling in the same direction as everyone else – and, secondly, you are likely to have a measurable impact on those things that the school most values. The key words to assimilate then are *alignment* and *impact*.

Now, your professional interests may only lie within the classroom and, understandably, you may want to continue to develop your expertise therein. It is fair to say, indeed, that the concepts behind whole-school leadership can be applied at the individual practitioner level. Teacher leaders are, for example, expert teachers who contribute to school improvement through activities such as curriculum development, bid writing, coaching others and the like. [26] Although this type of leadership is perfectly valid and valuable in its own right, we are going to focus on leadership and management development that goes beyond the scope of the classroom to take in the entire organization and its associated stakeholders.

So, when you look out across the school landscape do you see gaps in provision? Is there, for example, a key piece of relevant work that needs to be done but has been left because it isn't an immediate whole-school priority? Perhaps a new government initiative has come along which needs someone to lead it? Has the grapevine informed you that a colleague is seriously stretched and would appreciate support from anyone prepared to help out? These kind of scenarios offer you a chance to find a niche, or a small special space that you can call your own, within the organization. This unique space will become your vehicle for working more strategically across the school and, crucially, because it is 'yours', you can develop the role as you see fit without having to worry unduly about getting in the way of other initiatives. There is, however, a key point that you might like to bear in mind: it is preferable to find a niche that is outside your normal role and routines so that you get a chance to acquire new knowledge, work with 'new' people and learn new skills. You can use the niche activity to develop your strategic leadership capabilities such as: setting a strategic direction, aligning people and the wider organization to that strategy, translating the strategy into action and intervening when appropriate.[27] These are exactly the kind of activities that differentiate operational and strategic roles within the organization and which you would otherwise have limited opportunity to explore.

You might argue, however, that you don't need to find a niche in order to develop these strategic skills. Perhaps you have successfully led a department or team, you already have strong leadership capabilities and you shouldn't have to take on any more work. This is an entirely understandable response.

However, a department can be thought of as a 'silo', or a stand-alone component, running vertically through the organization. In other words, as long as you've got students and staff you can operate regardless of what's going on in adjacent vertically standing silos. There are, however, different leadership and management challenges – which require a different, though complementary, set of skills, knowledge and personal attributes – to be faced when working across the silos. Finding a suitable whole-school niche is a step towards identifying and addressing the whole-school challenges.

Perhaps the most obvious type of niche to look for is a pastoral post or a cross-curricular role such as a subject co-ordinator. There are, of course, pros and cons with such responsibilities. Two of the pros, apart from gaining a TLR (teaching and learning responsibility) point, or the support staff equivalent, is that you get to see work going on in other 'silos', and you will probably get dedicated time on your timetable to work on the responsibility. Beware, however, because these responsibilities also come with a big con in the guise of Ofsted. The new style Ofsted subject surveys mean they could, depending upon the national priorities agreed with the DCSF, come and inspect your whole-school responsibility, and guess whose door they will come knocking on? Thing is, Ofsted inspections, rightly or wrongly, are par for the course and you cannot expect to go through your career without bumping into them along the way.

So you're not afraid of Ofsted, and you happen to know that a cross-curricular responsibility is available, but it's one that no one wants to take on and, to make matters worse, it is in an area in which you have virtually no skills or knowledge. Well, you can either turn it down and wait for something more appealing to come along, or you can take the opportunity both to learn new skills and take yourself outside of your comfort zone. One might imagine that politicians face a similar dilemma when given new jobs to do – you might not remember Dr John Reid, but he is alleged to have said 'oh f—' when he discovered he was to become the new Minister for Health, during Tony Blair's reign as Prime Minister. John Reid knew that a significant challenge awaited him, but he got on with it nevertheless. This issue is about learning to love organizational agility – the ability to hop between successive, and increasingly senior, roles without either freaking out or stressing out, as skilfully demonstrated by John Reid and his political colleagues.

No Pay? No Way!

In order to secure a niche role, however, you might have to do something that many people will instinctively reject – you might have to do it without getting any extra pay, at least in the first instance, if there isn't a specific role vacant within the management structure. More work and more responsibility with no additional pay, surely not? Yes, afraid so. But it is critical that you look to play the 'long game' – securing a role on the senior leadership team isn't about instant gratification. Your rewards will come, and they will undoubtedly be generous, and you have to trust that your senior colleagues will reward your efforts. But you will have to 'front-load' on the commitment front and therefore give before you get. If you're thinking 'no way because my school will take advantage of my good nature', maybe you have misunderstood the purpose of what we're doing here – attempting to secure a senior role in the shortest possible time. If you wait until a paid post becomes available: a) you might have to wait a very long time; b) you might not get the post anyway; because you won't have been: c) learning the appropriate new skills/knowledge; and d) demonstrating your commitment to the wider school. Look, it will be hugely impressive if you've got the ability to spot an opportunity and have the intrinsic motivation to follow up by volunteering your services. Finding a niche in this manner demonstrates not only your commitment but also your ability to adapt to meet the needs of the organization.

There are all kinds of potential variations in this model – you might instead join working parties or work on special projects. It is the underlying principles, however, which are important, and not the specific mechanism through which they are realized. The key messages are: contribute in a way that will improve the performance and results of the organization and do something outside your usual role and routines in order to broaden your professional horizons.

The Pursuit of Extraordinary Performance

Let us work on the assumption that you will find a way to make a meaningful contribution to the wider organization. We are now at the point where we need to introduce the concept of standards. We'll talk about this in more detail in Chapter 4, but if you are to make a direct contribution to the performance and results of your organization, you'll have to do a 'good' job, at the very least. If someone said you had done a 'good' job on something, you might well go home that day very pleased with yourself, and understandably so.

However, and there's no easy way to say this, 'good' isn't good enough, not least because 'good' is the enemy of 'great'. Most people settle for a 'good' life and most organizations become quite 'good' at what they do.[28] Our tolerance for 'good' performance is endemic, unless we're concerned with airline safety. Then we demand world-class standards of performance – 99 per cent will not do![29] The thing is, if we want to create a world-class organization, we must aim for consistently 'outstanding' performance. Good performance will arguably maintain the status quo, whereas outstanding will raise the bar and set new standards of delivery. What we need, then, is a shift in expectations because good will just not do anymore.

Wouldn't it be fantastic if we had an entrepreneur within our ranks to help us deliver outstanding results? We know that entrepreneurs are driven self-starters who take calculated risks in the hope of big financial returns. They are obsessive about becoming successful and are, consequently, passionate about their mission. Entrepreneurs are results orientated, they don't take 'no' for an answer and they do whatever is necessary to get the job done. But they are also capitalists and mainly interested in enriching themselves; the size of their bank balance is a headline measure of their success. There are not, of course, many people working in education who are aiming to become rich – public sector service just isn't about personal gain. Wouldn't it be useful, however, to have all the attributes of an entrepreneur minus the ravenous appetite for personal financial enrichment? Just imagine what might be achieved! Welcome, then, the entrepreneur's close cousin, the *intrapreneur*.

There are a group of trail blazers within both the public and private sectors that might describe themselves as intrapreneurs. The crucial difference is that they work to build transformational teams, services, markets, structures, products and the like, from within their organizations by drawing upon the organization's resources, rather than resources for which they are personally liable – so they're not likely to lose their house or other personal assets as an entrepreneur might. However, make no mistake, these intrapreneurs are innovators, risk-takers, change-agents and visionaries.

You may recall that globalization will pose some considerable challenges for education in the coming years. Challenge invariably leads to opportunity for those who are prepared to behave as an intrapreneur – those who will learn new skills, keep an open mind, think outside-the-box and take a risk. Are you, then, going to take your niche role and begin building from within your organization – quite literally begin building schools for the future – not necessarily the physical structures, but a new BSF pedagogy? If you choose to do so, you have an opportunity to change the world along the way.

The question is, if you'll excuse the common vernacular, are you up for it? If the answer is 'yes', it will be virtually impossible to keep you off the senior leadership team. If you can't quite see yourself as an intrapreneur, you can still make progress through the traditional routes, but the price you'll pay will be time. Either way, let's be really clear here: 'Just about *anyone* can be a key protagonist in building an extraordinary business institution.'[30] And if *anyone* can build an extraordinary business, why can't *you* build an extraordinary school? So let us not agonize, or wring our hands, as we contemplate the discomfort that may come our way, let us instead get down to work and build with gusto.

Here, though, is an imponderable to consider. It is certainly possible to learn the practices that make an entrepreneur/intrapreneur successful, but it is unclear if those same practices are teachable.[31] As discussed in Chapter 1, there is no set body of rules to transmit from teacher to learner, but there are various characteristics and behaviours to adopt. You will have to learn to shape the leadership and management principles to fit your own unique environment and circumstances, if you are to build an extraordinary organization. The truth of the matter is that entrepreneurs, intrapreneurs, outstanding leaders, are neither born nor made, they are instead *self-made*.[32] This is why personal mastery is so important – you have the answers to the myriad conundrums facing your organization, you fundamentally know what must be done, but you must create your own effective solutions.

Vision

You might therefore start your building work by doing something else that most people instinctively shy away from. You are going to articulate what you stand for and where you see things going. You are going to develop a vision of the future and you are going to share your vision as you begin work in your newly secured niche. Now, before we get into this, let's not hear any groaning! Some sadly misguided people go around 'vision bashing'. Let us be absolutely clear about this; they are wrong to do it.

As it happens, virtually all leadership and management theory identifies vision as a core component. It is important to share your vision because it shows that you have a sense of direction, that you 'stand' for something and that you want to lead your team/organization to a better and brighter future. Furthermore, a vision statement, or a mission statement for that matter, creates a frame of reference by which people will govern themselves.[33]

So, great leaders are passionate, they fire the imagination and have an unshakeable belief that a better future is within grasp. And by describing that brighter future, your vision necessarily spawns a dissatisfaction with the present because, suddenly, there is a disparity between the current reality and the shiny future. This disparity generates 'creative tension'[34] and unleashes the energy required to drive forward the reforms needed to make the vision become a reality. Additionally, your vision will help you to speak with a compelling and distinctive voice;[35] a voice that will secure the commitment of others so that your 'personal' vision becomes a 'shared' vision – a vitally important step for transformational leadership. Your vision will also serve to reorientate and reinvigorate you when things get tough, as they invariably will. Make no mistake: 'The common denominator of success is a strong, empowering, guiding, inspiring, uplifting purpose.'[36]

There are, however, ways and means of sharing your vision and you might want to avoid the evangelical approach. The key is to share your vision and not to preach or impose: 'The leaders who fare best are those who see themselves as designers not crusaders.'[37] For some people the strategy begins and ends with a written vision statement. There is a place for written statements, but alone this will be insufficient to move things forward. The secret is to 'be the message'.[38] In other words, ensure that your own words and deeds consistently reflect the vision; lead by example.

It is, incidentally, important to distinguish between visionary leadership and charismatic leadership. Jim Collins and Jerry Porras argue that a high-profile and charismatic style of leadership is absolutely not required to create a visionary organization.[39] And consider the following comment from Peter F. Drucker: '. . . charisma becomes the undoing of leaders. It makes them inflexible, convinced of their own infallibility, unable to change.'[40] This means, contrary to what you might believe, you don't need to be ostentatious in order to become a highly successful leader. Building an outstanding organization requires visionary leadership and not a public performance, and your leadership ambitions are not doomed if you happen to have a fairly reserved character. As Bennis and Nanus point out, charisma does not *cause* effective leadership, but may be the result of effective leadership.[41] So quiet determination is quite enough!

In order to achieve the alignment we discussed earlier, it is important to ensure that your vision for your niche role resonates with that of the school. If you find that your vision instead clashes with the school's, and you cannot reconcile the two, it might be telling you something about your long-term prospects within that organization. Similarly, you may find yourself within an organization that is institutionally hostile to change; where the prevailing winds bring only ridicule, derision and disrespect to those who might presume to innovate. We might, then, consider Peter F. Drucker's advice which, in a nutshell, goes like this; if innovation isn't welcomed, don't waste your time and effort trying.[42]

Perhaps the school can't cope with an intrapreneur in its ranks because it simply hasn't got the capacity, in terms of time or material resources, to make the kind of changes you'd like to see implemented – the powerlessness belief system in action at an institutional level. If you have a deep emotional attachment to your school, where leaving to seek more fertile ground isn't an option, you may well go out and 'find' the required time and material resources. Commendable though such efforts would undoubtedly be, they may but spawn other organizational objections to the realization of innovative practice – perhaps first the curriculum needs to change, perhaps complications with the timetable will need to be thought through, parental consultation may well be required, the law might need to be changed! And on, and on, until you give up on the idea of making any radical changes and thereby leave the 'steady state' fundamentally untouched. It isn't difficult to see how a term might slip away, followed by a year, followed by a decade even, without much moving forward. Indeed, the INet Futures Vision think-tank argues that we should be outraged at the slow rate of progress in transforming our schools.[43]

So you might face something of a paradox – you might work in a school that doesn't want to innovate, and yet feel compelled to stay, knowing that progress may well be excruciatingly slow. Indeed, you might be under the impression that, as a newly designated intrapreneur, you're going to save the school from its entrenched malaise – a mere click of your fingers will see everyone suddenly start to follow you. You may also believe that only you have the answers, because you're the only one trying to secure innovative practice. Wrong – nothing could, in fact, be further from the truth. This process is not particularly concerned with addressing perceived shortcomings within the organization; it is, rather, about you making an outstanding contribution for the bene- fit of the students and the wider community. Your role is not to put things right, but simply to make your own contribu- tion, to the best of your ability. So, you need to keep your ego in check because you do not want to antagonize your colleagues.

You may find that as your journey to senior management gathers momentum, your newly found enthusiasm and self- assured persona disorientate those who have known you for a while. At this point in the proceedings you need to 'ground' yourself, so to speak, and ask whether you are displaying the behaviour and characteristics associated with a 'Level 5' leader: personal humility, compelling modesty and a ferocious resolve to make your niche activity outstanding.[44] As your actions start to betray your leadership ambitions, you need now, more than ever, to display humility. You do not have to apologize for want- ing to secure a more senior role, or high standards of delivery, but it does mean showing genuine, heart-felt respect for the people around you, and acknowledging that without their sup- port your journey would be problematic, if not impossible.

Your next challenge is somehow, and this isn't easy, but some- how to build your niche activity into something more sub- stantial, until it begins to move up the whole-school agenda. Clearly this will not happen overnight, but seek opportunities to work other stakeholders, to secure additional resources or to link with other projects or activities. This is where your intra- preneurial building instincts come in because you are looking to extend your influence in order to have a greater impact on the performance and results of the organization. But the thing is, you'll never finish the building work because there is always more to do – it's like forever 'chasing the earth's horizon or pur- suing a guiding star'.[45]

Depending on your disposition, you might be inclined to dismiss this approach, somewhat derogatorily, as empire building – and you'd have a point. There are, however, a couple of important points to consider. For a start, if you are building an empire, it isn't at the expense of your colleagues – it is something you intend to build with your bare hands, so to speak. There are those who will undoubtedly play politics – the attempt to accumulate position and resource power in order to increase influence within the organization.[46] You are not, however, simply out to wrest control of what already exists from other people. At the end of the day, you are working to improve provision, to add value, for the benefit of the students and the wider community. This kind of activity within a school invariably means influencing the work of others, and if that means you're out empire building, well, so be it.

Depending upon your school, you might find that such building work is welcomed. Many schools deploy a distributed leadership model, whereby people at all levels in the organization are empowered to be leaders in their own right. In fact, great leaders are successful because they identify, sustain and inspire other talented people in the organization.[47] With distributed leadership practices come the freedom and the responsibility to get the job done without having to seek permission from senior people before making a decision. With empowerment, however, comes accountability. If you're trusted to get a job done, you are then held responsible for the outcomes, which is fair enough. Life wasn't always like this, however. Once upon a time there was a distinct lack of organizational democracy in our schools. You might, for example, find yourself reluctant to work for one Edward Thring after he declared: 'I am supreme here and I'll brook no opposition.'[48] Now, you might still see Zeus-like figures commanding and controlling the organization from upon high – one leader supported by a thousand helpers – but you'll probably, hopefully, find that such traditions are in decline. Indeed, as schools become more complex, it is simply not realistic to expect one person to lead the organization effectively.[49] And even if such a superhuman feat is sustainable for a prolonged period of time, the Zeus-like head can hardly have the long-term future of the school at the fore of her or his mind – they will retire or leave at some point and what then for the school? Will progress made simply fall back because the chief protagonist has left.

So, your mission is to find a niche role with enough potential to allow you to work across the school and have regular contact with senior staff. It can be incredibly difficult, not to say daunting, to break out of your established patterns and routines. However, it is absolutely essential that you do this in order to gain new skills and knowledge. Will it sometimes be challenging? Yes, of course. Will you sometimes make mistakes? Yes, because you're human. Making mistakes is part and parcel of professional development and provided you learn from your mistakes and resolve not to repeat them, there is no problem – put it all down to 'growing pains'.

As this chapter draws to a close, we might take the opportunity to reflect upon the thoughts of Peter F. Drucker. People grow in stature, according to Drucker, in proportion to the demands they make of themselves. If they demand little, they remain stunted. If people demand a great deal of themselves they become giants – and, get this, they won't expend any more energy than the non-achievers.[50] Demanding higher standards of yourself at work does not necessarily mean expending greater effort, but it does mean stretching your comfort zones, acquiring new skills, doing what needs to be done – as opposed to what you might 'like' to do – and building your psychological resilience. Do not therefore accept second best of either yourself or your organization.

Let us therefore move swiftly on and take a closer look at the world around us.

3 | Tell It Like It Is!

'Simplicity, clarity, singleness: these are the attributes that give our lives power and vividness and joy.'

Richard Halloway

This is a very special chapter of the book because we're going to discuss how you might work to develop a crystal-clear view of the world around you – a key competency for those who seek personal mastery and senior leadership. Developing this skill is imperative because the first task of a leader is to define reality.[1] You might be tempted to think that you have this one in the bag already, but we humans tend to impose our own biases on our perceptions of reality because, 'it is more convenient to assume that reality is similar to our preconceived ideas than to freshly observe what we have before our eyes'.[2]

As it happens, every action we undertake is a test of those assumptions, so if what we do goes wrong we need to ask why, modify our assumptions and try again. We therefore need the ability to see past the commotion of everyday life in order to examine the reality from which it springs. And transformational leadership will require a commitment to continually improve our understanding of that reality because, you see, 'reality rules' and it will not subordinate itself to the beliefs of a leader.[3] So, your attempt to build a great organization will be in vain if your fundamental understanding of the world is flawed.[4]

With this point in mind, let's attempt to gain an understanding of the nature of reality.

It won't come as any surprise to learn that the debate about the nature of reality, and what constitutes knowledge, is intense and protracted. Philosophers, scientists and those of a religious disposition have been debating these subjects for a millennium or two. Essentially, there are two significant points of view on the issue that are of interest to us. Firstly, you can argue that reality exists 'out there', as an independent entity. We can come to know this reality by tinkering and probing with measuring devices. In this view of reality we can establish objective theory, or universal laws, that are continually tested and refined, and ultimately confirmed or rejected. So, for example, the theory of physics that sees an aeroplane fly in one part of the world, applies to all parts of the world, and would indeed apply to other worlds in the universe – if only we could reach them! The people who tend to investigate reality in this way are scientists, and they tend to gather numerical data, or quantitative data, as it's known, from their investigations. It is important to realize, however, that scientists do not claim to know the 'absolute truth' about reality, no matter how apparently true a phenomenon appears to be.[5] It is also worth noting that even when things seem very logical and measured, as they do in science, there is still an emotional, human basis from which the process commenced.[6] Actually, it may yet turn out that the physical reality we think we know so well is but a figment of our collective consciousness.

Defining our knowledge and understanding of the world in terms of quantitative scientific endeavour is, however, just one approach. It is equally valid to claim knowledge of the world through social constructivism – that sounds like a horribly complex term, but it means simply this: we make sense of the world through our interactions with others. A social scientist deliberately puts the human at the centre of the research process and seeks to make sense of the meanings others have of the world by gathering and analysing qualitative data, such as interview transcripts, questionnaire responses and the like. Most social scientists would readily acknowledge that their understanding of the world is rooted in their own personal, cultural and historical experiences.[7] In other words, we each see the world through the lens of our experiences and it is therefore impossible to detach ourselves from whatever we have under investigation – there is, in fact, no independent or neutral point from which to observe the world objectively.[8] Learning and teaching are obviously grounded in human morals, values and ethics. Such aspects of the social world are not, of course, physical phenomena open to scientific enquiry. However, the social world is no less 'real' just because it does not lend itself to scientific enquiry.

We therefore have two very different, yet equally valid, approaches to knowing the world in which we live. But things can get really complicated because you might want to mix things up a bit. You might take qualitative data like survey questionnaires and interview transcripts and group emerging results together in order to perform statistical analyses. Researchers who do this are, in effect, 'quantifying qualitative data'.[9] Learning and teaching are qualitative activities that become quantified through the assessment and testing regime. This ultimately leads to the creation of statistical models of school performance such as CVA (Contextual Value Added).

This brief overview is a gross oversimplification of a vast and complex subject, but we can draw upon these basic principles if we accept the need to define reality in our organizations. You might, of course, reject the whole 'define reality' argument because learning and teaching are essentially moral and social activities for which measurement of any type is totally inappropriate. However, as an aspiring leader, you will be called upon to make judgements about the quality of the provision. You could, of course, formulate such a judgement on the basis of your subjective perception, but will that judgement be both fair and balanced? The answer is, invariably, no. An insightful leader will be aware of her own perceptions, values and bias, but will nevertheless attempt to form a judgement on the balance of the available *evidence*. The question is not whether you can avoid making formal judgements, as this is an inescapable dimension of leadership, but whether you can properly consider the 'reality' experienced by others, as well as your own.

So every time you ask a question of your organization, you are in effect adopting the role of a researcher who is out testing reality: How well do students achieve in subject x? Is the quality of learning and teaching 'good'? How effective is provision x? How do students prepare for their future economic well-being? You will, perhaps, adopt a broadly qualitative or quantitative approach, depending upon your ontological (the nature of reality) and epistemological (the nature of knowledge) beliefs. Either way, your findings will have to be both *valid* and *reliable*.

In a nutshell, findings which are valid represent what they were designed to measure. Let's say, for example, you design a survey to find out if students enjoy a particular subject and discover that: '83 per cent of students surveyed enjoy subject y'. Not a bad result, but how many students represent that 83 per cent? If we find that there are 100 students in the population who might have responded, yet only six did respond, and five of those six (i.e. 83 per cent) enjoy the subject, there's a problem! The validity of the survey would undoubtedly be challenged because the number of responses is insufficient to measure what it was designed to measure. Now, reliability is concerned with the consistency of a method of measurement. If we find that the results of a survey run weekly vary wildly, we may conclude that, as a data collection tool, it is unreliable. The fault may lie with the ambiguity of the questions, or the method of distributing the questionnaire, or the profile of the respondents (boys answering questions aimed at girls, or KS3 students responding to KS4-type questions). Better not to proceed with unreliable data.

Other obvious threats to the validity of your judgements might include, as mentioned earlier, those based upon subjective feeling: 'I don't think students make progress in class x because they always seem to be chatting when I walk in.' A further obvious threat to the validity of your judgements might come if you make unsubstantiated generalizations: 'The data show that Y9 students haven't made any progress in subject y, therefore the Y11 groups will be the same.'

If the evidence is questionable, so will be the judgements upon which it is based. It is therefore important to learn how to form judgements based upon reliable and valid data, so that your judgements are not called into doubt. You might, for example, look for multiple sources of corroborating evidence – a process known as 'triangulation'.[10] If you get the same basic message about a particular aspect of your provision from different sources, or different methods, your judgements are more likely to be both valid and reliable.

Okay, before we proceed any further, you might be thinking this is all a little intense and excessive – surely you don't need to launch a research project every time you ask a question? A good point, in all fairness. But school improvement work has to be based on an understanding of current strengths and weaknesses. If your judgements are both valid and reliable, because the data upon which they are based is valid and reliable, you will be able to offer a clear rationale for proceeding in a given direction.

The Process of Self-Evaluation

Within school we might bring judgements about the quality of provision together to form a process known generically as 'self-evaluation'. According to Ofsted, self-evaluation is designed to drive improvement by demonstrating to stakeholders that a school both recognizes its strengths and weaknesses and has an appropriate action plan in place.[11] As an aspiring school leader you need therefore to engage in self-evaluation activities appropriate to your niche role. And though you might not be an academic researcher when carrying out your self-evaluation, you won't go far wrong if you borrow their tools and guiding principles. Of course, it's very easy to say that but, in truth, delivering good quality, rigorous self-evaluation is challenging. It is time-consuming and complex, but it is worthwhile because you'll gain a deep insight into whatever aspect of the school you have under review.

At the whole-school level there exists a self-evaluation form (SEF), a document that summarizes your school's current reality. The SEF is basically an audit of the school's own perceived effectiveness and has probably been compiled by the senior leadership team with support from middle-level leaders. It might be a document that you've never seen, never perhaps even heard of. Well, now you have, and you need to get hold of a copy and read it through. However, the SEF is a sensitive document. When you read it you should get an immediate impression of the school's strengths and weaknesses and, obviously, you'll be able to identify individuals who might be responsible for those strengths and weaknesses – hence the sensitivity. Why would you want to read the whole-school SEF? Because you can use this document as a model of good practice and a template to follow for your niche activity. We are not however going to get into the specifics of writing an SEF document – this isn't an instruction manual after all, but you should know that it is a challenging task and you will need to secure support and guidance when it comes to the mechanics of the process. Such support is, I'm afraid to say, beyond the scope of this book. Sorry.

However, the whole point of self-evaluation is to evaluate the *impact* of your work on the performance of students, which ultimately means determining whether you're contributing to an improvement in achievement and standards. Just so we're clear on the difference between achievement and standards, consider the following from Ofsted:[12]

◆ *Achievement*: This is a measure of learners' knowledge, understanding and skills in relation to their capabilities. It reflects how much learners are challenged, the progress they have made and whether they are working to their capacity. Key here is the value that a school adds and whether learners are doing as well as they can.

◆ *Standards*: By this we mean the level of knowledge, understanding and skills learners reach compared with learners of the same age nationally. In secondary schools, they are most likely to be expressed in terms of test and examination grades; in primary schools, in terms of levels; in early years' settings, they refer to children's learning in relation to the early learning goals.

The concept of impact can be rephrased into blunt, and sometimes painful, 'so what?' questions: You've delivered this healthy schools initiative, but so what? Your out-of-hours learning programme runs three evenings per week, but so what? The 'so what?' question exposes our inclination to describe our actions, rather than assess the subsequent impact: the progress we've made towards meeting an objective.

The 'so what?' question also reveals an implicit assumption that doing something, anything, is necessarily a good thing. For example, 'obviously a homework club is having an impact'. Really? Assessing impact does not necessarily have to relate directly to improved attainment – actually, there's debate to be had about whether anything other than the quality of classroom delivery, prior attainment and socio-economic factors make a difference at all to attainment. Anyway, if participation in an enrichment activity leads to a group of students having improved relationships with staff, that is in itself an impact – even better if improved relationships can be linked to higher attainment. Your evidence base, in this example, might include reduced number of reported behaviour incidents, greater amount of time spent 'on task', improved rates of work and so on.

So where do you start, in terms of writing an SEF? Well, you start by accepting the need to tackle the task and not instead neglect it in the hope it will go away. It won't go way, not least because it is a cyclic process rather than a one-off event. Once you have reconciled yourself to the need to get the task done, you face an even more challenging issue that requires thought in advance of undertaking the actual procedure: self-evaluation must be conducted in the spirit of openness, honesty and trust – and you will need to highlight any barriers which stand in the way of higher standards.[13]

At first glance this may seem like a clear-cut case of stating the obvious. However, let us recall that it is easier to assume that our preconceived ideas match reality, than to freshly observe what we have before us. If this is indeed so, you will need to look carefully at what the available evidence tells you about the quality of your provision/niche role – bearing in mind the issues concerning validity and reliability we discussed earlier.

Hear the Hard Truth

If you are not prepared to engage in the process in an open and honest manner, you may end up clinging to faulty assumptions about the world despite overwhelming evidence to the contrary.[14] And though it might be uncomfortable to accept that shortcomings exist within your organization, your areas of responsibility, true leaders are not afraid to hear the hard truth.[15]

You might sometimes find that large swathes of your organization are clinging to faulty assumptions about the world. And get this, they won't take kindly to you shaking their 'collective delusion' – a key reason to ensure that your judgements are both valid and reliable. I am, as it happens, sensitive to the historical difficulties that middle-level leaders have experienced in terms of assessing the quality of such things as classroom practice. The collegiate approach historically adopted by middle leaders, combined with the notion of teacher professionalism, meant that monitoring and accountability were considered unacceptable.[16]

It should be noted, incidentally, that an unwillingness to accept the truth, as the evidence portrays it to be, is not a specific school-related issue; even governments are susceptible to this phenomenon. Back in 1961, American President John F. Kennedy, and a small group of advisors, supported an invasion of Cuba by exiles. The adventure ended in disaster and Kennedy later asked how they could have been so stupid as even to entertain such a venture. Charles Handy puts it down to 'group-think', a phenomenon which occurs when a close team stops listening to the advice of outsiders, starts to suppress dissenting voices, demands conformity and develops a false sense of self-confidence.[17]

The moral of the story is simply this: just because everyone within a group, a team or indeed an entire organization, asserts that something is true, doesn't necessarily make it so. Perhaps our top strategic priority should be to eradicate both individual and organizational self-deception.[18] Let us therefore be alert and keep the words of American writer and journalist Walter Lippmann at the fore of our minds: 'When all think alike, then no one is thinking.'

So, there might come a time when the evidence suggests that some issue or other needs to be dealt with. You've faced the hard truth, as the evidence portrays it to be, but let's be honest, reporting bad news to the boss isn't a lot of fun. There appears to be an unwillingness to discuss difficult issues in many organizations for fear of triggering a 'shoot the messenger' response. CEO (chief executive officer) disease, as Daniel Goleman describes it, occurs when people won't break the bad news and instead prefer obfuscation over clarity: 'I can never put my finger on it, because no one is actually lying to me. But I can sense that people are hiding information, or camouflaging key facts so I won't notice. They aren't lying, but neither are they telling me everything I need to know.'[19] Such 'strategic ambiguity', the deliberate effort to resist open and rational reporting and analysis, not only holds back school improvement work but can have unpleasant consequences if Ofsted sense that the self-evaluation process is glossing over important issues. It is far better to conduct an honest, open, self-evaluation process, than have Ofsted come along and criticize you for a lack of rigour.

So, it takes courage to 'face the data' and admit, for example, that some aspect of your provision is perhaps unsatisfactory, based upon the balance of the available evidence. But an organization's ability to confront the brutal facts is a key attribute that helps transform a merely good organization into a great organization.[20] We might therefore embrace the guidance of computer games company Electronic Arts, who invite us to 'Challenge Everything'. Not bad advice, even if it is designed to sell their products.

In God We Trust. All Others Must Use Data

So, depending upon your approach to gathering evidence for your SEF, you might end up with qualitative data – for example written statements, questionnaire responses, learner quotes, basically anything that tends to be non-numerical in nature. Otherwise you might collect quantitative data – basically data that is numerical and can be used in a calculation (a telephone number, for example, is a numerical piece of data, but would be meaningless as part of a calculation). Chances are, you'll simply gather whatever is to hand because you won't be treating the delivery of your niche role as an academic case study or quasi-experiment. The result might be a mixed bag of data types that need to be organized into a coherent picture. Both types of data constitute valid evidence for your SEF, but, rightly or wrongly, there tends to be an emphasis on numerical analysis. Perhaps it is 'more valid' than the qualitative data, although at least half of the academic community would probably, vociferously, disagree. It is possible to run tests of statistical correlation and statistical significance on factors related to your niche role – and those of you with a strong quantitative leaning might well do so – but it is not necessary in order to complete your SEF. Most numerical analysis will involve the use of percentages and ratio, a review of trends over time and reference to pre-prepared reports such as RaiseOnline.

Now, this is an opportune moment to briefly explore the issue of 'cause' and 'effect'. Earlier we discussed an example in which a group of students appeared to have improved attitudes towards learning, improved relationships with staff and an increased work rate, following their participation in an enrichment activity.

Even though it may appear that the two variables (participation in an enrichment activity and improved learning outcomes) are related to each other, it is very difficult to establish in the social world that one thing causes another, that we have causality. There may be, for example, factors outside school that are contributing to their improving behaviour, and which inadvertently have also prompted the students to participate in an enrichment activity. Because of issues such as this, it is extremely difficult to *prove* a link. Even if you are certain that a link exists, and have identified other factors that are having an effect, there may be many more hidden factors that you'll never find. So, it is unwise to claim that your interventions/

provisions prove some kind of direct causal link to an outcome, like improved attainment levels. Proof is an exceptional standard that would be difficult, though not impossible, to establish in such a social context. Scientists, incidentally, are in a better position to prove causality because they can more easily isolate and control the different factors associated with their experiments. We cannot isolate and control the variables, on ethical and practical grounds, and can only therefore suggest, imply or argue that a link exists, on the probable balance of the available evidence.

And if that little conundrum wasn't bad enough, here's another issue to get your head around – causality runs in both directions. In other words, perhaps it is the students' improved behaviour and attitudes that cause them to attend the enrichment activity, as opposed to the enrichment activity causing the improved behaviour! You may think you know which direction the cause and effect ran, but it is just as plausible to believe that causality ran in the opposite direction. You might think this is simply playing with semantics, after all the strategy delivered the desired results, so what's the problem? Well, by refining your understanding of the notion of impact you're learning to disentangle the many complex interventions that affect student attainment. You will, therefore, become more skilled at developing and analysing future strategies designed to improve standards.

Developing your analytical skills is obviously important because, firstly, you need to ensure that you are effective in your role and, secondly, once a senior leader, you will need to secure accountability from the teams that you manage. You can be certain that, if you're securing accountability, people will question your judgement, and the evidence upon which that judgement is based, as well they might.

Self-evaluation may appear to be a complex undertaking, but you should not be aiming to produce anything as extensive as the whole-school SEF. You should be able to pick out a theme from the whole-school version and elaborate so that your document flows from the whole-school master. As it happens, you might even develop a strand of evidence that would fit better in the whole-school version. Either way, a rigorous self-evaluation process for your niche role, that is broadly synchronized with the whole-school process, will be massively impressive and will put you on the right road to senior leadership.

From Data to Information

The self-evaluation process tends to raise more questions than it answers. If, for example, your niche role involves running an initiative to improve the attendance of a particular group of students and the data suggests, from a baseline measure, that there has been a 2 per cent improvement, what additional understandings can you gain? Who are the pupils that have contributed to the 2 per cent improvement? Why did they respond and are there similar students who might have responded but didn't? Do they belong to a particular sub-groups – e.g. boys/girls, those entitled to free school meals, students from ethnic minorities, pupils with special educational needs, and so on? So, just because you have data that indicates a 2 per cent improvement, you don't simply stop there and celebrate. You celebrate and then move on to the deeper analysis in order to secure further improvement. Reality testing means going beyond the first level of data to try and gain a deeper insight into the underlying issues.

Actually, something very important occurs when you begin to analyse data in order to gain a deeper insight into the nature and the effectiveness of the provision. You begin to transform the data into a much more valuable commodity, namely, information about the inner workings of your organization. When this information is based upon valid data, it becomes a very powerful to tool for explaining to others what's going on. The raw data is replaced with a narrative that is much more accessible for those who have neither the time, the inclination, the remit, nor the expertise to conduct the analysis for themselves. And, when you can construct that narrative, you can claim mastery of the data.

Of course, it is easy to imagine a scenario in which the link between the narrative and the supporting data is, at best, weak, or indeed non-existent. This is something absolutely to avoid when you conduct your self-evaluation. Firstly, don't be tempted to establish a fictitious link to the data because you'll get found out. Secondly, do not report invalid subjective feelings. You may very well 'feel' that there has been an impact, but where is the evidence to substantiate the claim? If you can't substantiate the claim with some data, either go and find some that does substantiate it, or else don't make the claim in the first place. This might seem a bit over-the-top, but the more unsubstantiated material contained within your self-evaluation document, the greater the threat to the validity of the process – and, as previously mentioned, if the self-evaluation process is invalid, it may lead to questions about the future direction of your niche role and, indeed, the wider organization.

There can be fewer higher-order skills more valuable to an organization than the ability to synthesize disparate data sources into one coherent story. It is valuable because this process allows you to see patterns emerge from the complex interactions between what you do (cause) and how well your students subsequently respond (effect). It is not, however, a skill that comes easily – it requires practice and discipline if it is to be mastered. Stephen Covey reminds us that few people know how to diagnose the health of an organization using data, never mind then to go and identify improvement priorities and appropriate objectives.[21]

Yet data analysis is critical to improving systems and processes, and it is only through the use of properly interpreted data that intelligent decisions can be made.[22] If the truth be known, however, school leaders have not been historically good at using data to inform whole-school decisions.[23] And yet the skills required to gather, interpret and chart data are neither complex nor difficult to master. But the very sound of techniques such as correlation analysis, frequency distributions, variance and mean is enough to strike fear into the heart.[24] In reality such data manipulation and exploration is not particularly difficult to grasp – definitely no rocket science involved!

Data is not, then, something you begrudgingly collect because you feel you have to, or have been told to, and it is literally meaningless until you perform some level of analysis on it. A superficial analysis will return superficial findings – why not go data mining and see what might be discovered? You are not, after all, a contestant on the iconic TV show *Catchphrase*, and you do not therefore have simply to: 'say what you see!' Things are not black or white and a snapshot rarely tells the full story: 'there is more to seeing than meets the eyeball'.[25]

As you engage with self-evaluation you will develop your thinking processes and spend more time interpreting problems before attempting to solve them.[26] The secret is to uncover the underlying simplicity of otherwise complex phenomena.[27] And let us not forget that the greatest threats to our organizations, and indeed wider society, come not from sudden events but from slow, gradual processes.[28] Sometimes you need to pay attention to the subtle as well as the dramatic.

So, following the self-evaluation process, you will discover that a number of priorities for improvement emerge. Everyone, no matter how outstanding the provision is, will have development points because there is no such thing as perfection. The key question always to keep in mind is: 'Would this be even better if . . .?'

The self-evaluation process is key, then, to helping you and your organization make further progress. You must therefore ensure that you have a very clear and concise understanding about where you currently stand before attempting to move forward. After all: 'It is not enough to do your best; you must know what to do, *then* do your best.'[29]

The next step is to translate the findings, the key priorities for improvement, into an improvement plan – so on we go!

4 | Deliver the Goods

'If we did all the things we were capable of doing, we would literally astound ourselves.'

Thomas Edison

There can be no getting away from the fact that as an aspiring school leader you have got to be able to 'deliver the goods'. There is no room on a senior leadership team for people who are all smiles and no substance. Of course you need to be personable, a team player, a reliable and trustworthy individual who is attuned to wider organization, but above all of these things – and *because* of these things – you must get results.

It is very easy to secure a niche role and do nothing to move things forward. Now, you might argue, you haven't got the proper resources or don't have enough time to get the job done. Frankly, the powerlessness belief system needs to be overcome for those who aspire to senior leadership. And so, while the ability to adapt and learn defines your potential for senior leadership, it will be the capacity to deliver results that ultimately determines whether you will be a success in the role – failure to translate intentions into tangible improvements will undoubtedly damage your credibility as a senior leader. The ability to deliver strategic objectives, to coin a macho-sounding cliché or two, sorts the 'men from the boys', 'the wheat from the chaff'.

Before you get started in your niche role, we need to think back to the earlier discussion about standards and ask where you are positioned on the performance continuum? Does someone need to micro-manage you, or are you an effective, motivated self-starter? Can you energize colleagues as both a team leader and a team player? Will you be able to sustain your initial enthusiasm, drive and energy, or will it fade until you find yourself doing the bare minimum required to keep your manager at bay? Will you be very busy, but perhaps not very productive, due to a reluctance to tackle the more challenging aspects of the role? And what might motivate you to maintain a high standard of performance once the initial burst of enthusiasm begins to wane? Pay and status would certainly propel most people forward in the first instance, but will that be enough to sustain performance over a prolonged period of time? Perhaps an appeal to our professional ethics would suffice – after all, not many people would want their performance standards to be so poor as to be branded unprofessional. And what about fear? Perhaps high standards of performance can only be sustained when we're afraid of the boss or the potential wrath of Ofsted.

Those who pursue personal mastery don't need to be motivated by external factors such as fear, salary and status. True, most people need to earn money in order to pay the bills, but the motivation needs to be fundamentally intrinsic. Money is a pleasant side-effect which arises from 'delivering the goods', and is not therefore a means to its own end. After all, would you be satisfied with a big job title and lots of cash if you were only given donkey work to do?[1] So, your motivation might be centred around tapping into your passions, establishing a culture of innovation and high expectations, or helping others develop as leaders in their own right – all key emotional intelligence competencies for successful leadership.[2]

World-class or Bust?

So, you might decide to deliver world-class standards and become an intrapreneur within your organization. But have you really got the bottle, the sheer gritted determination, to aim for outstanding delivery with all the blood, sweat and tears it will entail? Have you got the tenacity and resilience to strive for, and deliver, world-class standards? Before you leap to say 'yes!', just reflect momentarily upon that standard: cutting-edge practice, consistent delivery everyday, outstanding performance in every Ofsted inspection, national/international leader in the field. Now leap to say 'yes!' – now that you know what you're letting yourself in for. What an amazing standard to aim for, but why not? Someone has to be leading the field, why not you? Needless to say, you will need to develop a world-class vision to accompany your aspirations, and you'll also need the support of your family, friends and colleagues. But here's the thing; from now on 'outstanding' is the benchmark against which you will measure everything. If something you want to achieve isn't pitched at this level, it isn't pitched high enough.

If you feel this narrative is beginning to reach the realms of overbearing enthusiasm, it is because aptitude, motivation and optimism are the three most significant personal characteristics held in abundance by highly successful individuals, according to psychologist Martin Seligman.[3] So those of you committed to lifelong learning, and who happen to be in possession of a positive, unfailing, 'can-do' attitude, won't go far wrong.

Back to Reality

Now you have to be a bit of a pragmatist here. You won't, of course, walk into school 'tomorrow' and suddenly transform everything into outstanding provision; you are aspiring to meet this standard and it will take time to secure improvements. As a result you're going to have to live with the frustration that the organization isn't moving as quickly as you'd like.[4] But having decided to set such a high standard, you need to start working at an appropriate level in order to secure the results that you're looking for. In other words, you're not just going to pay lip service to meeting the standard, you're actually going to go and plant a 'beacon of excellence' in your school. And this is one of the reasons why you need to have rock solid self-belief, because without it you'll stumble at every hurdle. Without such a conviction, your vision of the future will be forever over the horizon, beyond reach, and you won't consequently realize your full leadership potential. But let's just remind ourselves that, while securing world-class standards will be challenging, it won't be as difficult as rocket science. You do not have to be a creative genius in order to lead innovate practice – yes, you need imagination and yes, a little creativity will go a long way, but the capabilities required are not beyond the ordinary, and certainly not within the realms of divine inspiration.

As it happens, what needs to be done will be blindingly obvious, though not necessarily easy to implement. The question you need to answer is this: are you prepared to step up and do it? What makes the process of securing world-class standards challenging is not the external barriers you perceive to be in the way, but the personal commitment to implementing the required changes.[5] So, the most amazing thing about choosing where to work along the 'underperformance to world-class' continuum, is just that. It's a choice that you make, and the choice is largely determined by your values, beliefs, motivations, skills, knowledge,[6] aspirations, self-esteem and self-belief – in other words, your 'mental model' of the world and your place therein. So, as like most things in life, you will basically 'reap what you sow'. If you make a half-hearted effort at your niche project or role, you'll get half-baked results. Your attitude to getting the job done is inextricably linked to results: you are your attitudes and your attitudes are you.[7] This is, in fact, a time-honoured principle. Two and a half thousand years ago, or thereabouts, Aristotle pointed out that: 'We are what we repeatedly do. Excellence, then, is not an act, but a habit.' If you set off with a burst of unsustainable energy you'll quickly run out of steam and drop back to doing the bare minimum, and complain that you are powerless; that you have neither the time nor the resources to get the job done properly. So you will have to pace yourself and build towards your vision. Great results come from generating momentum; taking steps forward, achieving results, energizing people around you and moving forward to the next cycle.[8]

A Quadrant 2 Existence

And thinking about powerlessness due to a lack of time presents an opportunity to introduce you to the virtues of a quadrant 2 existence. Sometimes we obviously feel overwhelmed by the challenges we face. Occasionally, you will come across a task that you find impossibly large or complex, and the nature of the task might mean that you can't ditch it, or delegate it. You might find, in fact, that you don't even know where to start, never mind how to get it finished. When faced with a potentially overwhelming task like this, the secret is to take a step back and not let yourself get all worked up – although that's sometimes easier said than done.

But, no matter how challenging, you need to begin tackling whatever job you have before you as soon as possible. Here, then, is some beautifully simple advice to help get you started: 'do first things first and do one thing at a time'.[9] This is a great management principle, but it's not of much use in the real world. In these busy times, we need a very practical tool to help us prioritize our workload. Say 'hello' to Stephen Covey's time management matrix (TMM).[10] Though it has a rather intimidating name, the TMM is a brilliantly simple and highly effective tool that might just change your working life. Well, that's a bold claim, so let's hope it lives up to the billing.

Over the years we've become more sophisticated in terms of managing our time. Notes and checklists have been supplanted by diaries and calendars. But we now need to prioritize our time in terms of our values.[11] As Covey points out, effective time-management practice of today is concerned with enhancing relationships and accomplishing results. If we therefore identify mid- and long-term objectives and only work on those things aligned with our values, we are more likely to realize our goals. We can do this by categorizing activities according to urgency and importance. Urgent matters obviously demand immediate attention, but they may not necessarily contribute to our overall goals – it's that feeling of busyness you sometimes get while not actually achieving anything of significant value. Of course, important work is significant, but it needs to be properly prioritized. The matrix below can help us do just that:[12]

	Urgent	Not Urgent
Important	*Quadrant 1 (Do now)*	*Quadrant 2 (Plan to do)*
	Emergencies, crises, demands of others, impending deadlines, fire fighting, staffing issues	Planning, designing, investigating, networking, thinking, modelling, creating, system/process development, strategy
Not Important	*Quadrant 3 (Reject and explain)*	*Quadrant 4 (Resist and cease)*
	Trivial requests, ad hoc interruptions, distractions, pointless routines or activities	Surfing the Internet, computer games, daydreaming, doodling, chatting

If you want to be effective in your role stay away from quadrants 3 and 4, because 'urgent or not, they aren't important'. Instead, try to live your professional life in quadrant 2 because from that place comes vision, perspective, balance, discipline and control.[13]

From Theory to Action

You may recall that the point of finding a niche was so that you could work strategically across the school and develop new knowledge and skills along the way. To ensure that you are able to do this, we are now going to look at some practical management strategies to help you point your organization in the right direction.

Firstly, there is a bit of a conundrum for competent operational people, across both public and private sectors. Competent practitioners tend to get promoted into management roles – some less than competent people also get promoted to stop them doing damage at the operational end! But for the most part it is the competent who make progress. There is perhaps an assumption that because someone is, say, a highly capable classroom practitioner, they can also lead a team or manage a project effectively. However, a good classroom practitioner will not necessarily make a good manager or senior leader. There just isn't a seamless continuation between the two types of role; though admittedly the two competencies are linked. And presumably there would be no need for NCSL leadership training courses like Leading from the Middle and NPQH if it were possible to make the transition seamlessly.

It would, however, appear to be a matter of common sense to promote those who have been successful in operational roles to more tactical, strategic and managerial roles. Now, once in a more senior position another issue arises: the leadership facet of the job is distinct from the managerial facet. In other words, an effective leader might happen to be a terrible manager, and vice versa. So, although leadership and management competencies are often thought to be synonymous, they are indeed distinct. Sometimes you will wear your leader 'hat' and at other times you will require your manager 'hat'. When you operate in leader mode you are shaping a vision of the future, setting a strategic direction and selling your ideas to others. When you are in manager mode you are using systems, monitoring targets and directing a team. It might be useful to think of the difference as follows: 'Stability is the goal of what is often called "management". Improvement is the goal of leadership.'[14] Peter F. Drucker goes one better by eloquently noting that 'Management is doing things right; leadership is doing the right things.' That said, you should know that there is no universally accepted distinction between these two roles – academics and practitioners alike are embroiled in heated debate and it doesn't look like it's going to be settled any time soon!

Let us not, however, get distracted by the debate and instead contemplate your future leadership and management activities. It is important to recognize that 'sorting things out' as part of your current or future management role does not, in itself, necessarily constitute professional management activity. In other words, you might get a job done, but can you identify a theoretical framework that underpins your actions? Chances are, you've had very little leadership and management training and therefore practise what is known as experiential learning – learning through the experience of doing. This is a perfectly reasonable and legitimate strategy, but there is no theoretical context underpinning the practice.

Is it important to have a theoretical framework to guide your practice? Well, that would depend on your perspective. If, arguably, it is important to have theories to underpin teaching practice, such as, for example, Gardner's multiple intelligences and Vygotsky's zone of proximal development, it is also important to acquire an understanding of management principles such as TQM, matrix management and six sigma. We might therefore reflect upon the words of Deming: 'Experience by itself teaches nothing.' We might also be persuaded that abstract concepts drive creativity by facilitating unconventional action. In other words, you might be led by theory to try something you would never have otherwise considered. You cannot, after all, consider alternatives without a background concept in your mind.[15]

So what then of your leadership skills? If your team or your niche role simply 'is as it is', without a 'higher purpose' that extends beyond its immediate and obvious function, you are arguably not practising professional leadership. At best, you are simply 'at the front' of the group. Perhaps your leadership and management style can therefore be summarized as 'the organizer at the front'? We have seen, however, that motivating people, setting performance standards and articulating a vision are key leadership behaviours. If you do not display these behaviours, what exactly does leadership mean to you? Getting paid more than others to do a particular job? Having more knowledge and experience than others in order to solve problems?

It might sound harsh, and it could be that you've performed well up until now, thank you very much, but ask yourself if such an informal approach to school leadership and management practice will facilitate a transformation in standards? Let us therefore work on the assumption that a more systematic, theory-driven approach to leadership and management will bring about an improvement in organizational performance. Let us also work on the assumption that transformational leadership actually requires strong management capabilities – not an assumption that everyone shares, as we'll see later.

So if leadership and management practice is to become more formal, how might that work? We have, so far, talked about the principle of breakthrough innovation – the idea that an intrapreneur can work within an organization to create novel ways of giving value to stakeholders.[16] If breakthrough innovation is *revolution*, then adaptive innovation is *evolution* – the process of securing incremental improvement to what you already deliver. Now, both processes may be in full swing in your organization and you may need to be involved with both types at different times. If, for example, you are working on a project to introduce new practice using ICT, that might count as breakthrough innovation. On the other hand, if you also belong to a pastoral team that is seeking to improve attendance by speeding up a monitoring system, that might count as adaptive innovation.

So, how about this, as a framework to underpin and formalize your future adaptive innovation management practice: How about a commitment to secure, incrementally, continual improvement in the quality of your existing provision? In Ofsted speak, that might mean moving through the judgement grades: Inadequate > Satisfactory > Good > Outstanding. But delivering outstanding services isn't the end of the road because the responsibility of those who have outstanding practice within the organization is to support – through a combination of coaching and mentoring – provision at other points on the scale. If everyone follows this improvement process, the entire organization has the potential to become outstanding. But that isn't the end of the road either, because an outstanding organization then has a responsibility to support other organizations in their attempts to improve. See how that works? Definitely not rocket science. So, does this model sound familiar? Advanced skills teachers (excellent teachers)? Federations? School improvement partners? This kind of practice, or 'system leadership', has been shown to be effective, among headteachers at least.

In practical terms, it means translating your exhaustive self-evaluation process, and the newly identified areas for improvement, into a school improvement plan that's specific to your niche role. It is important to note that you are not going to write a 'development plan'. A development plan is about developments and developments do not necessarily translate into improvements – labelling it an improvement plan might not, of course, lead to improvement, but it is the shift in perspective and the associated language which is important. Anyway, there's no point doing something to develop provision if, in fact, the actions do not lead to improved outcomes for your learning community. Incidentally, you might also want to move away from the idea of a departmental development plan, if you're still using that terminology. Apart from the problem with the word 'development', the concept of a departmental plan reinforces the notion that you're only interested in improving that 'silo', or department. In the same way that 'no man is an island',[17] no department is an island, and your concern now is for the improvement of the school as a whole, and not just your patch. You may think this is simply playing with semantics, but the use of new language helps to shift the thinking from *department* to *school* and from *development* to *improvement*. Not insubstantial changes, you'll no doubt agree?

There exists a management principle that you might use to underpin and formalize your improvement work, known as total quality management (TQM). This is, basically, a set of systems, methods and tools to help an organization manage its resources more effectively in order to achieve success.[18] When an organization subscribes to the principles of TQM it commits itself to a continuous journey towards excellence.[19] This translates into pursuing an unrelenting focus on the continuous improvement of four areas: personal and professional development, interpersonal relations, managerial effectiveness and organizational productivity.[20] The goal is to get things right first time, every time. TQM processes should therefore be holistic: they need to permeate every aspect of the organization, every relationship and every process.[21]

The adoption of TQM is linked to the self-evaluation processes discussed in the last chapter. So some significant questions must be asked about the way things are done. How, for example, are quality goals devised, pursued and measured? How do management systems respond to quality issues? Are training programmes geared towards delivering performance that will meet or exceed customer expectations?[22] It is really important to also recognize that a commitment to quality goes much further than simply improving organizational systems and structures. It is a commitment linked to personal mastery: that is, the need to continually improve ourselves both personally and professionally.[23]

Now, the father of modern quality management practices, Dr Deming, demands that the commitment to quality management begin at the top of an organization. Indeed, when the Ford motor company was struggling and crying out for help in the 1970s, Deming refused to meet representatives until the request came from the top guy, the chief executive.[24] If the senior leadership team are not committed to the rigorous pursuit of quality, the endeavour to continually improve organizational performance is likely to result in cursory, superficial effort. However, that shouldn't put you off applying the principles of TQM to your niche role, not least because you're leading by example and intend to plant a 'beacon of excellence' in your organization (assuming, of course, that your school doesn't already deploy TQM practices).

You've probably guessed that the principles of quality management have their roots in the private sector and, though you might think it should stay there, let us look momentarily at the basic principles in action. Let us say, for the sake of argument, that we have a production line manufacturing a car engine component. If we were to assess the quality of the component, we might take random samples and examine the component's performance against various standards, such as, heat tolerance, or strength, or whatever. If an assessor finds that the part has a defect, it's too late because thousands of these things are pouring off the production line and they're all useless. Better, then, not to inspect the end product, but instead look to improve the processes that give rise to the product in the first place. If the processes are fundamentally sound, the end product is likely to be fit for the purpose. So, the old way was 'to inspect bad quality out', whereas now we seek to 'build good quality in'.[25]

How is this relevant to education? Well, we can use our own quality review method, self-evaluation, to both identify and improve ineffective provision (i.e. intervene to ensure that we 'deliver the goods' before it's too late!). And, incidentally, if we are conducting our own internal quality inspections, we might well ask if we can make Ofsted redundant. Nice idea, but Ofsted's role is to verify that a school understands its strengths and weaknesses. In other words, they will quality assure the quality assurance. Perhaps it is clear that you, our aspiring leader, will find it very useful to acquire the skills of an Ofsted inspector.

Assessing standards against national quality frameworks is one such way to develop these skills. You might, for example, turn to external benchmarks such as: Investor in People, International School Award, ICT Mark, Leading Aspect Award, Inclusion Mark, Matrix Standard, and so on. The significant benefit of securing these awards is that they give you an opportunity to determine the current state of your own provision, as compared to the standards laid out by the awarding body. If you already meet or exceed the specifications, great, you can secure an award that confirms your good practice. These external, and objectively assessed, standards also lend credibility to your service delivery and might give you a little breathing space when Ofsted next come to visit. So, why not use quality awards as a tool to move provision, incrementally, through the Ofsted grades: Inadequate > Satisfactory > Good > Outstanding?

However, in the final analysis, good quality service is whatever your customer tells you it is, hence the need to listen carefully to your stakeholders' requirements. And though the idea of customers or consumers in education might be unnerving, we must think of students and their parents/carers as consumers of an education service.[26] Not least because the students themselves recognize that they have rights and expect services to be tailored to meet their individual needs.[27] But will we take them seriously as customers? Will we try to find out what best suits their needs? Can we adapt our practice to suit their wants? Shall we gather feedback, and do we discuss the implied contract, the fundamental transaction: 'if we do this, will you do that in return?'[28] These questions also apply to our internal customers – our colleagues and the multi-agency stakeholders who are integral to the operation of the organization.

Overcoming Obstacles

So, let's assume, for the sake of argument, that you've secured a niche role and you intend to improve some aspect of the school. Imagine, therefore, that you've decided to apply for a quality award because it offers a good opportunity to review processes and policy. As you work towards assessment, however, you begin to realize that the workload is heavier and more challenging than you initially expected and, worse still, you've discovered that the cost of assessment is going to be significantly higher than you first thought.

Now, overcoming obstacles like this is at the nub of the matter, as far as leadership and management practices are concerned. You'll recall from Chapter 1 the very simplistic model of leadership which boiled down to strategy followed by execution. On this occasion we have a strategy (apply for an award) but execution is problematic (expense and challenge). If, however, you commit to achieving an objective, you must see it through, regardless of the obstacles.

True, you may need extra time to get the job done, but persistence will result in success. Let us recall that 'whatever you do, deliver the goods' is the bottom-line capability of a senior leader. Powerlessness due to a lack of resources, whether money or time, should not be a barrier to achieving goals and meeting objectives. It is easy to give up, but outstanding leaders and managers find solutions – to paraphrase Collins and Porras; resilience in the face of adversity is the signature of greatness, whether it be in a person, organization or, indeed, a nation.[29] You must, then, become determined and resilient to the point of obsession. You must use those skills that marked you out as a potential senior leader in the first place, the ability to learn and to adapt, to find a solution. A solution might not, of course, be immediately to hand, but resources have a habit of turning up when you are out searching and luck tends to favour the persistent.[30] You may find, for example, that you suddenly identify a specific funding source that you hadn't previously noticed because it wasn't particularly relevant to your needs. Perhaps you will identify new skills among your team, skills that can create capacity or devise new solutions to previously intractable problems. So roll up your sleeves and bring the issue to heel, whether that be through lateral thinking or sheer hard work.

This example demonstrates an instance where the skills and knowledge you possess 'today' are insufficient to solve the problems of 'tomorrow'. In other words, a new problem has unexpectedly arisen and you aren't fully prepared to deal with it. Well, basically, it's tough. If you start something, you have to see it through to a satisfactory conclusion, rather than just abandon it. If a problem arises, you have to solve it. It's an uncompromising message because, if you can't finish what you start, you'll never build the momentum required to achieve a breakthrough to world-class standards. Instead, you will forever languish around the mediocre mark surrounded by the detritus of incomplete or insubstantial projects, and will ever be left wondering what might have been.

Alignment and Action!

You will, of course, have to take action in order to deal with problems as they arise. As it happens, there can be few words more important to leadership and management theory than the word 'act'. Ready for the mandatory *Oxford English Dictionary* definition: 1. take action; do something. It will come as no surprise to learn that many a large corporation has based their entire ethos around the idea of getting a job done, and it goes something like this: To 'act' and get it right is ideal. To 'act' and get it wrong is not ideal, but is acceptable. To not 'act' is intolerable.

How odd, you might think, that it is better to do something wrong than do nothing at all. But the ability to 'act' is critical and you'll be amazed at how many people find it deeply problematic. You can be certain that many organizations which hold great ambition and high ideals also have a heinous inability to translate their lofty intentions into concrete actions.[31] The problems arise when the required action involves doing something new, because new means different, and different has the potential to take people out of their comfort zones. Unlike you, most people have not learnt to control their self-talk through the process of personal mastery and therefore retreat to 'safe' territory rather than face the discomfort of the unknown.

So, come on, hands up: have you ever written a development/ improvement plan and then simply left it in a cupboard gathering dust – having never once acted on the action points? A little witticism then to make you smile: Three frogs are sitting on a lily pad and one decides to jump off – how many are left?

The answer is three – *deciding* to do something and *actually* doing something are very different![32] There is little point in talking passionately about what you want to do, what needs to be done, if you cannot follow it up with action. It is, then, absolutely critical that you learn to translate planning into action, as this is the key to improving organizational effectiveness.

Coming back to the ultra-simplistic school leadership model discussed in Chapter 1: strategy and execution. The ability to act is obviously related to the execution element of the model. Could it be, do you think, that the secret to delivering outstanding provision is simply for all to act in a timely manner upon a common plan? In others words, ask each individual within the organization to: organize and execute around priorities.[33] As concepts go, this one is beautifully simple, and perhaps blatantly obvious, yet fiendishly difficult to implement. Achieving such 'strategic alignment' in our schools – whereby everyone acts upon agreed priorities – appears to be of critical importance and yet particularly challenging to achieve.[34] In fairness however, the 'alignment' problem is prevalent everywhere.

Covey invites us to answer the following questions, in order to determine whether we have an alignment issue: 'Is our mission statement a constitution? Is it the supreme law of the land? Does every person who comes into the organization make a commitment of allegiance to that constitution? Is every program, every system, even our organizational structure, subject to the constitution?'[35] The response to these questions usually tends towards the negative and so we have an alignment problem.

One might begrudgingly align and consequently act in the manner of a petulant teenager who has been goaded into doing the housework. But the quality of the outcomes in this case probably won't lead to improved provision. People have to be motivated to act because, fundamentally, they are aligned to the organization's vision of securing a better future. So the secret is to secure action that is driven by a desire to excel, rather than in response to coercion or some impending disaster. It is indeed something of a misconception to suppose that people will only act in a time of crisis – e.g. an imminent Ofsted inspection, dire predictions of exam performance, a looming budget deficit, a threat from competitors. It just so happens that for many organizations such crises tend to focus the mind more sharply than the vision set forth by leadership.

Anyway, returning to the issue of 'action'. It's not about performing any old actions, of course. The actions need to be relevant, hence the self-evaluation process and the corresponding improvement priorities. Of course, we might find ourselves with a list of unpalatable and uninspiring tasks to complete, but as Peter F. Drucker points out: 'We must identify what *has* to be done, as opposed to what we would *like to do*.'[36] In order to be effective, we have to put aside our personal preferences and tackle instead those things that we know will have an impact on the organization, no matter how disagreeable they might be to us personally. One of the differences between those people who have tremendously successful lives and those that don't is concerned with just this issue: 'The successful person has the habit of doing the things the failures don't like to do. They don't like doing them either necessarily. But their disliking is subordinated to the strength of their purpose.'[37] In other words, their mission is so compelling that it overwhelms any unpleasant tasks that might be encountered along the way. Even so, let's be absolutely clear here; undertaking operational types of task like unblocking toilets, filling dishwashers, emptying bins and the like, actually count as pleasurable tasks, if you are doing them to avoid the challenging strategic activities (like self-evaluation, for example), which you know ought to be done in order to move the organization forward.[38]

It is perhaps tempting to think that the only strategy to execute is a detailed master plan from which there should be no deviation. Not so. In fact, opportunism and serendipity are just as important to the process. Make no mistake, you need a plan, but not shackles or a straitjacket. If opportunity knocks on your door, be prepared to let it in. If the opportunity later turns out to be a distraction, or an outright hindrance, it obviously needs to go, but experience will soon teach which to grasp and which to let sail by. And within the spirit of opportunism comes experimentation. When new approaches are tried, new outcomes arise. And some such outcomes will be desirable and others less so. The key to keeping things moving forward in your organization is to try different approaches and keep what works.[39] This 'emergent strategy', as it's properly known, allows the future to, well, emerge within the boundaries of strategic intent – that is, within the broad themes and areas of development that are compatible with the organization's core values.

Now, after reading all that, here's the irony. Even though you know how important it is to 'act' – to identify priorities, devise strategic plans, to test reality, to listen carefully to your customers – the bet is that you'll put this book down and continue exactly as you have always done. You might have done the same thing after attending a training course – left with good intentions, then carried on as though it had never happened. It seems that exposure to new knowledge is not enough on its own to trigger a change in practice – follow-up support in terms of coaching makes a change in behaviour more likely to happen.[40] You have been exposed to new knowledge but might not have immediate access to professional support within your organization. So you have to learn to act under your own direction. Now, there may well be legitimate barriers that prevent you from implementing some of the suggestions in this book – a heavy teaching commitment, other responsibilities and commitments, a hectic social and family life.

Know this, however; regardless of how challenging you find the process, if you don't change your professional behaviour, adopt some of the leadership and management practice discussed here, and consistently meet ever higher standards of delivery, mediocrity will stalk you relentlessly until the end of your working life. Again, let's be clear. You can still do very well and have a fulfilling career, but the art of transformational leadership may forever elude you. Yes, the message is blunt, but it is an indication of how centrally important the issue is to your leadership aspirations. There is no time for procrastination, excuses or hesitation. Act upon those things that need to be done to improve the organization, and do it now. The school is your metaphorical playground and you can do pretty much anything you please, provided it fits within your organization's core values and purpose. So assume you have the freedom to act. If you see something that needs to be done, do it. If you have in mind some really innovative practice, do it. Talk to others beforehand, if you feel it necessary, and then do it. As sportswear company Nike advise: 'Just do it'. And if you get it wrong, you can always apologize later. It is, after all, better to apologize after the event than to seek permission beforehand.

Even if you are inclined to 'act', you might find that others don't share your enthusiasm for either innovation or the additional effort. While it may be frustrating, the fact of the matter is, outstanding whole-school performance will require '. . . willingness and commitment at all levels in the organisation to align their actions and make modifications as required to meet the desired goals'.[41]

Though it can be frustrating, the important thing to recognize is that one individual, yes you, can make a big difference. No matter how impossible the task might seem, you can get things moving in the right direction. So plant that 'beacon of excellence' and let it stand as a shining example of what can be achieved if the bar is set high, if you translate careful planning into focused action. There is no reason to become frustrated or despondent, because you will know that you've done the very best you can given the circumstances. Your intrapreneurial spirit will mean that you go on to plant other 'beacons of excellence' and eventually the wider organization will start to take notice and a new organizational culture will begin to emerge. It is for this reason that you need to build momentum by continuing to 'deliver the goods'. A virtuous circle of accomplishment will eventually form because success begets success. And as the results start to impact upon the organization you will become an attractor within the system – people and resources will be drawn towards you because you will be known as a person who can get the job done to an exceptionally high standard.

It is, of course, one thing to pontificate about the importance of translating intention into action, but another thing to offer concrete help to get you started. And sometimes it is just plain difficult to know how to get started. So, I'd like to introduce to you a practical management tool: the PDSA cycle. This cycle is also known by various other names: the PDCA cycle, the Shewhart cycle, the Deming cycle and the Deming wheel. Basically, it is a four-step cycle designed to improve the quality of a product or service – the principles apply regardless of service, sector or product. Believe it or not, this management tool has been around for decades, since the 1950s in fact, when Dr Deming first introduced the concept to the Japanese during the postwar era. So, the cycle goes like this: Plan, Do, Study, Act.[42]

◆ Stage 1 (Plan) involves scrutinizing a process and deciding which changes might bring about an improvement in provision. Once you've decided which changes to make, people and resources need to be organized.
◆ Stage 2 (Do): you now make the changes which should be small-scale in nature.
◆ Stage 3 (Study): well, you simply observe the effects of the change on the process.

◆ Stage 4 (Act) demands that you make any necessary adjustments, look for unexpected side-effects and identify further improvement priorities that can feed the next cycle.

Again, the PDSA cycle is not rocket science, but it might just provide you with enough structure to begin the process of transforming your organization.

Measuring Performance

Having the 'freedom to act' is all well and good but such action requires an assessment of impact, else it will be difficult to know if you're making a difference to your community. Once you have your development priorities, you need to identify a small number of key objectives to focus upon. Now, you were promised this book wouldn't be a tepid instruction manual, so we're not going to explore the intricacies of action planning, but we will briefly look at the concept of SMART objectives and key performance indicators (KPIs) – very quickly, promise.

An objective is, put simply, a planned goal, something you're aiming to achieve. Once you have decided which objectives to aim for, following the self-evaluation process, you can identify action points to move you towards the objective. If your objective is to ensure that every Y11 student creates a 'progression file' to detail their planned route into further education or employment, your actions might involve creating a tracking spreadsheet, interviewing each individual student, arranging employer/college visits, and so on.

The stated objective, 'to ensure that every Y11 student creates a progression file', isn't, however, entirely SMART. The objective is Specific (the planned outcome is clear) and it is Measurable (every Y11 student), it is also Achievable (within the capabilities of both students and the organization) and Relevant (to both student and the wider organization). It is not, however, Time-bound because there is no achievement date for the objective. You are strongly encouraged to set delivery timescales for both action points and the broader objectives in order to create a sense of urgency and to prevent drift.

If you wanted to track progress towards meeting the objective, you might count the number of students who successfully complete the process. This is what we might call a key performance indicator, or a KPI. It is a headline measure used to quantify progress towards the objective – it's not, you'll note, a measure of the actions taken (such as setting up spreadsheets, meeting with employers, or interviewing students), but of progress towards meeting the overall objective (all Y11 students with progression files). The KPI is not therefore a measure of the amount of work you have done, but is rather a measure of the intended impact upon your students. So, setting up spreadsheets and meeting with employers are 'actions', but until the students create a progression file, these actions will have had no impact! If all Y11 students create a progression file, you can claim, though not necessarily prove, that the impact of your actions was substantial. Self-evaluation serves, of course, to assess whether the work you do leads to better outcomes – it is possible to be very busy (carrying out lots of actions) but not very effective (have little impact)!

This next suggestion is a matter for debate, but how about we focus only on the measurable aspect of the objective? And why? Well, brace yourself for a major revelation. When you can precisely measure your progress towards meeting an agreed objective, you can make a claim about your overall effectiveness. In other words: 'I said I was going to do x, and data y demonstrates that I have. Now refute that if you can!' The more 'fuzzy' the objective, the less certain you can be in terms of your progress and, consequently, the more open your evidence will be to interpretation and potential criticism. Put simply, when you say you've 'delivered the goods', you need to produce a 'dispatch note' as evidence. You are not, then, necessarily accountable in terms of how specific an objective is, or how achievable, and so on. The only thing you're judged on is the output measure, the impact on student outcomes. Your objectives, M-objectives (if that's what we might call them – 'M' for measurable), can then be broken down into specific action points and compiled into an improvement plan. Take note, however. Some school improvement plans read like the technical specifications of the international space station! The secret is to keep it simple – less is definitely more!

Careful planning translated into focused, disciplined action, can it really be that simple? Maybe it is that simple, but maybe you don't like the idea of measuring your performance against objectives? Although there is a huge debate to be had over performance measures in education, there must be, arguably, some bottom-line measures of performance for everyone – a 'scoreboard' of some descriptions is essential for evaluating success.[43] Yet when we consider the moral dimension of schooling, in terms of, say, transmitting cultural and moral norms to the next generation of young people, we cannot easily set targets and measure progress for such outcomes.[44] Very true, of course. However, my suspicion is that the journey to outstanding delivery requires the recording and monitoring of strategic measures. It is the only reliable and verifiable way to ensure that planning is converted into actions, and that actions have a desirable impact upon standards. Remember: 'you are what you measure'.[45]

Taking Risks – Feel the Fear!

Setting out to deliver strategic objectives, via PDSA cycles, or any other method for that matter, is a something of a risky strategy. What if things go wrong? What if something totally beyond your control trips you up and you find that no amount of adaptation or innovation will put things back on track?

You might argue that we educational types are, on the whole, a reserved and risk-averse bunch. Can we only ever expect to take tiny, incremental, safe steps forward because of our fear of the consequences of getting it wrong? Should we throw caution to the wind and set about taking giant strides? True, giant strides mean great risk, but they also mean potentially fabulous returns for our learning communities. Is it better, then, to have disastrous consequences resulting from a calculated risk, provided no one gets hurt obviously, than to do nothing for fear of failure? Some organizations see failure as an inevitable part of their ongoing development – something would be seriously wrong if things weren't sometimes going seriously wrong – as Johnson and Johnson say: 'Failure is our most important product.'[46] We have to be really clear, then, about the question of taking risks – the 'do nothing' scenario is, downright, utterly, intolerable. It is far better to have a mess to clean up than to shy away from taking a risk for fear of getting it wrong.

If your inclination is to avoid the big risks, we're back to the tiny, incremental steps. However, in terms of your niche role, there is a way to spread the risk and it relates to the collaborative nature of senior leadership. If you can see an opportunity to potentially secure a fabulous return for your community, share the decision to take the risk with the senior leadership team. This isn't a cynical ploy to cover your back, but it is both an opportunity to work closely with the team that you want to join and a resource, in terms of skills and experience, for you to call upon should something unexpected happen.

Will the senior team really be comfortable with a disastrous consequence arising from a calculated risk? Well, they will consider the risks with you in advance and if they feel the risk is too great they will advise/instruct you not to proceed. Of course, if your school proceeds with a big risk, and disastrous consequences ensue, that's just hard luck for everyone. Learn from it, get over it and move on. You should know, however, that spectacular failure brings its own rewards – through the crucible of the experience new learning and new understanding will emerge.[47] So the very nature of risk-taking means that things will go wrong: the greater number of risks taken, the greater the probability of something going wrong. But don't let a setback or two put you off – you will find strength in adversity. So you may not always achieve the outcome you were expecting when you take a risk, but you'll always learn something new![48] And if you do learn something from a misadventure, you will be forgiven for getting it wrong, regardless of the consequences. So be bold, go frighten yourself a bit – safe in the knowledge that if you leap, there's a good chance that a net will appear![49]

Time to Reflect

As we bring this chapter to a close, let us pause and reflect for a moment, in case you're now sat thinking something to the effect of, 'I haven't come into education to do this! Adaptive innovation, TQM, self-evaluation, PDSA, M-objectives, key performance indicators – what's that all about?' This is the distinction between the operational side of the organization – classroom delivery and its associated activities, and the tactical/ strategic side of the organization. It is perhaps now clear why learning and teaching and leadership and management are distinct, albeit linked competencies. And having read this far you may seriously question the role of such leadership and management theory in education – ultimately you may decide to disregard much of what you have read and carry on regardless. You may, in fact, know successful and charismatic leaders who haven't the first clue about, nor the faintest interest in, the theory, but still manage to get great results. Perhaps the strength of their interpersonal relationships, the depth and breath of their experience and their own energetic, passionate belief in what they do is enough to lift the entire organization to higher standards of performance. Yes, enough of this performance and quality nonsense – children are not, after all, car components spewing forth from a production line! But how will improvements be sustained when that charismatic leader leaves the organization?

You probably won't be surprised to hear that there is a strong anti-managerial bias within some schools, the focus instead being upon the moral dimension of the educational process. In all fairness, anti-managerial sentiments have also been prevalent in the corporate world for the past 70 odd years, so it's hardly a school-specific phenomenon. However, I'm sure it's obvious where I personally stand with regards to the rather crude moral versus managerial dichotomy, but just so we're clear, the working assumption is that the '. . . strengthening of management knowledge and skills is essential to the ability of leaders to achieve the vision set for their schools, both locally and nationally'.[50]

Simply 'pointing the way', or becoming 'emotionally attuned' to others, or empowering and motivating people to develop a 'can-do' attitude, as a highly charismatic leader might, seems to lack substance without an accompanying managerial dimension. Let us also bear in mind that somebody, somewhere, in the organization has to manage the processes – especially as school services become more complex over time. Leadership capabilities are not, therefore, a substitute for management skills and they should not therefore be disassociated from each other – despite protestations to the contrary. It is unrealistic to assume that as a leader we can pass the 'management buck' because we find the work unduly trivial, irrelevant, tiresome, difficult, distracting or dull.

Else where would the 'management buck' stop if leaders at all levels did the same thing? Well, consider the current trend. Business managers, who tend not to be qualified teachers, are now handling such things as personnel, finance and premises, because those kinds of activities distract senior leaders from the core business of learning and teaching. But various aspects of learning and teaching need to be managed too, such as assessment data. So, we appoint non-teaching data managers to take away the burden of handling and analysing large quantities of data. This is, of course, perfectly legitimate and logical because teachers, well, teach! And so students and staff are better off as a result of this diversification. But the lines of demarcation between the roles of senior leaders (typically qualified teachers) and senior managers (sometimes non-teachers) begin to blur – and aren't you guys, business and data managers, also school leaders in your own right?

Leadership capabilities and management skills must therefore go hand-in-hand, though they may be deployed in different ways, and be of a different calibre, depending upon your seniority and your particular responsibilities. We find, however, that existing training programmes tend to focus around the development of leadership capabilities, thereby leaving the management skills to be developed by magic. As you might have noticed, I haven't covered in any kind of depth the practical details surrounding the application of, say, total quality management (TQM) to your niche role. Beyond a description of the broad principles, you're left to work it out for yourself. This is a clearly insufficient strategy if we are to pursue, in any kind of sustainable way, world-class standards. At least, however, you are now aware that such techniques exist and have shown themselves to be effective at raising standards across many sectors.

If, then, we see the management aspect of our professional life distributed across the organization, alongside the leadership dimension, better outcomes are assured for everyone. While such distribution appears to be the right thing to do, we aren't likely to move away from hierarchical management structures any time soon. After all, whether leadership and management activities are distributed or not, someone still needs to carry the formal accountability. And even flattened management structures still consist of a hierarchy, though there tends to be a greater emphasis across the horizontal dimension of the organization.

So, while our leadership capabilities enable us to draw up a blueprint, our management skills provide the tools to translate the plans into improved provision. Yes, we are both the architect *and* the builder. Perhaps, then, we should reject anti-managerialism in all its forms and instead usher forth a management renaissance across the sector, similar to that which swept first across Japan in the 1950s (due in large part to Dr W. E. Deming), then later across corporate America and Britain in the 1980s and 1990s. Though many, of course, will angrily disagree and instead put other concerns, such as the moral purpose of the schooling process, far ahead of management practices.

Actually, I think you can have a morally focused, yet managerially orientated school – the two paradigms are not necessarily mutually exclusive. And here's the real irony: when properly conceived, management practice is hugely liberating and empowering – professional autonomy is enhanced, not diminished. People thrive when there's clarity of purpose, consistency of approach and explicit accountability. And creativity isn't stifled by managerialism; strong systems actually facilitate innovative practice because solid foundations are conducive to experimentation. Within strong management structures we can, indeed, find shelter and a degree of certainty as we seek progress in these turbulent times.

And so we can summarize what is meant by 'deliver the goods'. Does it mean, do you think, that you're to go out and ruthlessly pursue your development objectives by converting planning into action? Does it mean developing the discipline to avoid distractions by ensuring a laser-like focus on key objectives? And what to do about that provision that does little, if anything, in terms of impact upon students? Are you aiming to become a lean, mean, educating machine – an Olympic athlete in education land? Or is 'fuzzy' okay – and what then of your measurable outcomes? Is it therefore time to proceed with disciplined action? Do we need the courage to confront the brutal facts of reality? Are we brave enough to realize our vision by modifying organizational structures, changing relationship norms, reshaping systems and raising performance expectations?[51]

Whatever practice we decide to adopt – regardless of the founding principles, whether they be emotional intelligence, moral imperative, or management practices – the secret to long-term success appears to be linked to the consistent, disciplined, application of whatever processes that subsequently emerge. But how do we know that we've designed the right processes, that we're doing the right things? By rigorously testing reality and engaging with adaptive innovation, of course.

This chapter has explored what it might take to deliver world-class standards in our education system, though I honestly don't pretend to have any definitive answers. The question is, however, are you willing to entertain these ideas, find your own solutions, and then adapt your practice accordingly? The real killer question, actually, is this: Can you apply the rigorous, disciplined practice to your day job as well as your niche role? Can you get the 'bread and butter' stuff, the mundane and routine work, lifted into the realms of the consistently outstanding, even when no one else is watching? Where do you currently rate your everyday performance on the standards continuum? Can the principles of total quality management, PDSA cycles and M-objectives apply here? And do you have the courage to challenge the practice you might consider to be good, on the grounds that 'good is the enemy of great'?

5 | Make Like You're the Boss

'The only real training for leadership is leadership.'

Antony Jay

Despite the title of this chapter, you're not about to be encouraged to go strutting around your school with an air of self-importance! No, afraid not. However, we are going to contemplate your wider responsibilities to the organization, and also consider the implications for other people when you, an aspiring senior leader, are looking to get things done.

Absolute Power Corrupts Absolutely

We're going to start by talking about *power*. This is not, however, a topic often discussed in polite company. As a leader, you do hold power, and in fact we've alluded to the concept of power, or the lack thereof, throughout this book, but have not as yet discussed the issue directly. So, what do we mean by power? Well, put simply, it is the capability to get something done.[1]

Most people consider the idea of holding power over others to be somewhat vulgar and therefore resort to euphemisms when discussing the subject. When we use the power we hold we might instead say that we are 'exerting influence', and when we acknowledge that someone has power over us we say they are 'in a position of authority'.[2] Charles Handy, a management guru of some considerable stature, identifies four distinct varieties of power to use when you want to achieve a goal. To start with there is *resource power,* which quite obviously is concerned with having control over some vital aspect of the organization – this includes, incidentally, non-physical resources, such as time-bound processes and information. Secondly, you might have *position power* – this is often the source of power that goes with a senior leadership role. Thirdly, there is *expert power* which, as you might expect, confers a particular kind of authority based upon your special skills and aptitudes. Now, there's something slightly unique about expert power: it is effectively given by the people over whom you might yield it.[3]

And if we may dally with the vulgarity of power a short while longer, you may realize that this book is founded upon the principle of developing your leadership and management expertise – in other words, your *expert power.* You will become a credible leader because you can do the day job (i.e. your teaching role, or non-teaching equivalent) and deliver strategic objectives within your niche activity. Of course, there are those who may use bluff and blag to secure position power. However, anything other than expert power can be taken away at the drop of a hat. Once you have developed these leadership and management capabilities, they are yours. And only you can destroy them through neglect.[4] So, anyone thinking about attempting to secure a senior leadership role without also developing the ability to 'deliver the goods' might find the position untenable in the long term. Similarly, anyone who becomes an expert but fails to continually update their skills, knowledge and world view may also find their future somewhat precarious.

The last kind of power that Charles Handy talks about, negative power, isn't concerned with getting things done at all. It is, rather, about stopping things from happening in the first place. Those who can't, or won't, make a positive contribution; the bored, frustrated, the marginalized, the petty and the impotent, may decide to use their negative power in order to have a detrimental influence on some process or other. After all, even the humblest of us can stop something, even if we haven't got the ability to start something.[5]

Stephen Covey, in his book *Principle-Centred Leadership*, takes a different perspective on power and leadership by looking instead at why people choose to follow. In short, people follow for three reasons. Firstly, leaders exercise *coercive* power – in other words, they yield the 'big stick' and followers follow out of fear for the consequences. Next comes a type of transactional leadership, called *utility* power – leaders exchange money, status, security and the like with followers. In return, leaders get talent, time, support and energy from the followers. Finally, comes *legitimate* power which, argues Covey, is centred around a commitment of the follower to the vision and mission proclaimed by the leader. People follow because the vision is compelling, because there is a sense of belonging, because there is an opportunity to contribute to something of significance.[6] Interestingly, broader academic research has shown that leadership tactics which involve persuasion, consultation, collaboration, and inspirational appeal tend to be most effective. Ingratiation, exchange and apprising are moderately effective and applying pressure is least effective.[7]

The message would appear to be clear: exercising legitimate, expert power is the way to get things done. Those leaders who attempt to coerce, those who have a tendency to bark orders in the belief that aggressive behaviour instils fear and respect among their colleagues, are sadly misguided – it just tells everyone that they can't handle pressure, or that they're emotionally unstable, or they're just rather badly behaved. After all, leadership is not about abusing people, but is instead about persuading people to work together in the pursuit of a common goal.

However, you may occasionally come across someone who abuses their position and power by dominating and, in extreme cases, humiliating people within the organization. You might be interested to hear what Daniel Goldman and his colleagues have to say about such leaders: 'They create wretched workplaces, but have no idea how destructive they are – or they simply don't care. Some . . . are more subtle, using a surface charm or social polish, even charisma, to mislead and manipulate.'[8] These leaders are the archetypal 'smiling assassins', who are sadly devious by nature and toxic at heart. Make no mistake, many of these people lack compassion, humility and empathy. And, as it happens, the ability to empathize with others, that is to see and feel things from someone else's perspective, and to do that with sincerity, is the most critically important interpersonal skill to develop as a leader.[9] Dale Carnegie argued, towards the end of his book *How to Win Friends and Influence People*, that an increased tendency to empathize with others may prove to be a hugely significant stepping-stone in your future career development.[10]

Now, there is a 'tool' that might help us develop this capability. The Six Thinking Hats method, devised by Edward de Bono, provides a structure that helps us to explore an issue from various, parallel, perspectives.[11] This method of thinking is supposedly more advanced than the simplistic argument/counter-argument method that has served Western civilization, in particular, rather well for these past two millennia or more. The idea is to approach a problem from six different perspectives – each perspective uses the metaphor of a different coloured hat. So when a group of people are together discussing a particular issue, all need to be aligned to the same coloured hat: that is, using the same thinking strategy at a given time:

◆ White Hat represents information: What questions should we ask? What information do we need? What data is relevant?

◆ Red Hat serves to explore emotions: gut reactions, displeasure and dislikes, with no further justification beyond how something makes you feel.

◆ Black Hat is assigned to critical thinking as we commonly know it: What is the logic of this? Does this align with our values?

◆ Yellow Hat thinking concentrates on finding value, identifying the potential benefits and looking for the positive aspects.

◆ Green Hat thinking demands that we seek alternatives and be creative.

◆ Blue Hat serves to co-ordinate and define a focus: Why are we meeting together? What are we trying to achieve?

The Six Hats method provides a framework to help us sustain a dialogue rather than win a rhetorical argument. It provides an opportunity to 'think always in terms of the other person's point of view, and see things from that person's angle, as well as your own', as Dale Carnegie puts it.

There Is No 'I' in Team

Throughout this book we've talked about your role and developing your skills. Well, all of this discussion around 'you' is, actually, a bit of an illusion. It's not about *you* at all, but it is about *people* and the *team*. It's an old cliché, but there really is 'no "I" in team' and recognizing that you need others to achieve strategic objectives will mark a significant step forward in your professional development.[12] And because we have an obligation to work together, there are seldom times when we are truly independent or autonomous – we may have freedom to act, but we should never lose sight of our wider responsibilities to the team, to the goals we're trying to achieve as an organization. We should therefore remain aligned to the greater good because, in truth, we can't achieve world-class standards as individuals pursuing our own interests and agendas. The pursuit of our own concerns leads inescapably towards mediocrity.

Now, the leadership and management concepts we've talked about in this book thus far apply equally well to the work of a team. There needs to be a strong team vision, resilience and alignment. The right people need to be in the right team roles and those people need to be testing reality and meeting the required standards. Ultimately, your challenge is to build a collaborative team culture where mutual respect and open dialogue, combined with high performance expectations, become the norm. But some people find teamwork incredibly challenging and instead choose to stand apart. Sometimes this choice is driven by ego; an individual may not want others to discover their shortcomings. Sometimes the choice is determined by an individual's belief that they can do a better job if they're just allowed to get on with it. But it is important to recognize that you can't do everything yourself.[13] The Hero Leader model is simply unsustainable for this very reason. There is neither the time nor the capacity for any one individual to deal effectively with the complex leadership and management challenges of today.

Of course, we may empower others and find that a superstar emerges. That person may have the potential, indeed, to overtake those in more senior positions. Through his work as a leadership consultant, John Maxwell argues that some leaders are prone to bouts of insecurity and perceive the growth of others to be a threat to their own position.[14] As a consequence, such leaders surround themselves with weak individuals so that they can dominate and maintain control. There are two issues here. Firstly, such practice obviously panders to the insecurity of an individual and fails to prioritize the needs of the wider organization. Secondly, such practice is plain wrong – as a leader you have to be magnanimous. You have a responsibility, as a leader, to develop the potential in others, even if that means watching such individuals make rapid progress and perhaps even surpass your own capabilities.

So, when it comes to dealing with others, you are either 'inside the box'[15] and therefore treating people as though they are objects, with little consideration for the person and their needs or aspirations. Or else, you are 'outside the box' and therefore leading with integrity – honestly matching words and deeds with no desire to manipulate, deceive or control.[16] Truly outstanding leaders, then, remain reliable, consistent, approachable and upbeat no matter what they might be dealing with. There will be no crazy mood swings, no unpredictable Jekyll and Hyde type of behaviour. This is what you have to model if you're to inspire confidence and loyalty among your colleagues. Consistent, optimistic and self-confident. Easy!

And if you are to lead a team well, you need a deep determination to improve your ability to deal with other people.[17] You must, therefore, put *people* at the top of your leadership and management agenda. School leaders have not, however, embraced the 'people agenda' as ardently as they might over recent years. It is the key, however, to recruiting top talent, retaining key individuals and developing skills across the organization.[18] You must therefore make 'people' a key strategic priority.

Empowerment, Obviously?

Throughout this book we've talked often about empowering people and distributing leadership, whereby formal structures are augmented by a network of leadership activities stretched across the organization.[19] Now, the concept of distributed leadership is very much in vogue at the moment. However, there is some doubt that distributed leadership practices have a direct impact on student attainment levels. Yet it does feel like the right thing to be doing; we want to be empowered to do our jobs. We shouldn't have to constantly check with managers before making decisions that are commensurate with our role and responsibilities. And there is evidence to suggest that organizational change and development are enhanced when leadership is broad based and where teachers have opportunities to collaborate and engage in innovative activities. So let's be honest, who would enjoy the prospect of being disempowered? No, let's distribute leadership, let's empower our teams to make decisions and take action!

This is great in principle, but consider the following from Peter Senge: 'If people do not share a common vision, and do not share common mental models about the business reality within which they operate, empowering people will only increase organization stress and the burden of management to maintain coherence and direction.'[20] So empowerment cannot be unconditional. It has to be negotiated, it has to be planned and regulated else we risk spontaneous misalignment (where unplanned collaboration comes to a halt), or even anarchic misalignment (the active rejection of what should be done) – both of which will obviously have consequences for the organization.[21]

If empowerment must come with 'strings attached', what conditions might we expect to see? Well, Covey advocates a win-win agreement between manager and subordinate. The agreement represents a mutual understanding regarding expectations, results, accountability and consequences.[22] Securing accountability and administering consequences is not an aspect of professional life that most people enjoy tackling. Beware, however, because when there is no accountability people start to lose their sense of responsibility and begin to blame circumstances and other people for poor results.[23]

And we do tend to be quick to blame others. We'll see later that people are seldom to blame when things go wrong (it's usually the system that's at fault), and we must therefore take care to avoid criticizing people, no matter how justified we think the criticism might be – even if someone completely disobeys a direct instruction. This is such an important point that I'd like to retell a story that appears in Dale Carnegie's book, *How to Win Friends and Influence People*: American President, Abraham Lincoln, had ordered a general to attack enemy forces and thereby bring a swift end to the American Civil War. Lincoln issued the order and waited to hear news. Astonishingly, the general disobeyed the order and prolonged the suffering. Did Lincoln criticize the general for his disobedience? No. Instead he empathized with the general's situation on the ground, distraught though he was at the missed opportunity. If Lincoln can be so magnanimous under such circumstances, surely we can follow his example under less trying conditions. As Carnegie says: 'Any fool can criticize, condemn and complain – and most fools do. But it takes character and self-control to be understanding and forgiving.'[24] Things do go wrong, people don't live up to our expectations for various reasons, but yellow hat thinking (finding value, identifying the potential benefits and looking for the positive aspects) and a determination to see things from other people's perspective will help you to gain deep insight and understanding into the issues. When dealing with others, 'seek first to understand, then to be understood'.[25]

Actually, many of these interpersonal skills are associated with the realm of emotional intelligence (EI), a concept popularized by psychologist Daniel Goleman in the 1990s. There has been a growing realization over recent years that the emotional dimension of our school role is significant. Indeed, the art of transformational leadership emphasizes the part played by emotions, values and symbolic behaviour. In essence, EI is concerned with four key themes:

◆ Self-awareness – the ability to reflect upon the state of your inner emotions.

◆ Self-management – the ability to manage emotions, adapt to change and remain intrinsically motivated.

◆ Social awareness is concerned with your ability to read and react to other people's emotions.

◆ Relationship management deals with the ability to motivate, inspire and influence other people.

If you have self-control, empathy with others, high levels of self-motivation, and can comfortably interact with others, you probably have a high EQ – or emotional quotient. And if you can manage conflict and secure alignment, you are demonstrating your emotional competencies.

However, it is important to realize that developing your emotional intelligence is no substitute for securing the other leadership and management competencies described throughout this book; you must master those key skills too and you absolutely must be able to 'deliver the goods'. In other words, you need to be secure in both the emotional and the rational dimensions of the role, though those with an anti-managerial bias might well disagree. You might, then, want to reflect on your own level of emotional intelligence and answer questions like: How aware are you of your own emotional state and the effect your emotions have on others? Do you, for example, 'transmit' stress to your colleagues because you feel it yourself? Are you prone to outbursts of anger? Are you impatient in your dealings with others? Is sarcasm, cynicism, or spite part of your interpersonal repertoire? If this is indeed so, a return to Chapter 2, and the discussion surrounding personal mastery, might be required in order for you to both identify and eradicate the mental models that give rise to these damaging traits.

As it happens, there are also a number of techniques associated with NLP, or neuro-linguistic programming, that you may want to investigate further. NLP is designed to help you to establish more effective interpersonal relationships, although the underlying 'science' is perhaps questionable. You should realize that an entire industry has developed around the delivery of NLP, and those who facilitate the training make bold claims concerning its effectiveness. Will NLP training change your life and your career prospects? As with many aspects of this book, you're advised to keep an open mind and challenge everything.

Whether you decide to engage with NLP training or not, the issue of continuing professional development is, of course, extremely important. As we noted in Chapter 1 there is a potential headship crisis facing schools as the present post holders begin to retire. Actually, according to the National College of School Leadership (NCSL), there is a real 'war for talent'[26] going on across many sectors, both public and private, as organizations scramble to secure their future leadership and management needs.

Are you, then, looking after your own professional development needs? And if you're not consciously planning your ongoing developing, who will do it for you? Do you have a career development plan, with indicative timescales? If school leadership is to figure significantly in your future, there does need to be, as we have already seen, a theoretical underpinning to your practice. Can you secure a place on a National College of School Leadership course? Are there other academically focused courses run by local universities that might appeal? Such qualifications obviously represent long-term commitments, but they may just transform your practice, your organization and your career.

To Motivate, But How?

Anyhow, the way you respond when someone does not live up to your expectations might well be determined by your assumptions about human nature and motivation. Let's see, then, if you subscribe to theory X or theory Y assumptions devised by Douglas McGregor in the 1960s.[27] Theory X suggests that people work as little as possible and are not actually very bright. They tend to lack ambition, dislike responsibility and prefer to be led. Such people are self-centred, indifferent to the organization and resistant to change. The best way to motivate such individuals involves coercion, threats and punishment.

Theory Y, on the other hand, suggests that people are not by nature passive, indifferent, or resistant to change, but have become so because of their working environment. Even so, when people are committed to organizational objectives, they will assume responsibility and be self-directing and disciplined in their actions. If managers take their responsibilities seriously, they will create an environment which enables people to take the initiative and develop their intrinsic potential; in short, they will be distributing leadership responsibilities across the organization.

This is of course an oversimplified view of organizational life and each theory represents an extreme end of the scale. In case you're wondering, McGregor subscribed to theory Y assumptions because he felt this outlook, and its associated approach to getting things done, was more likely to achieve the desired results. Either way, improving employee performance is a central leadership concern[28] and, to paraphrase the author John Buchan, the task of leadership is not to put greatness into people, but to elicit it, for the greatness is already there.

So, depending on your perspective, people are either lazy and disengaged or deep reservoirs of untapped potential. We can, of course, take comfort from the suggestion that appropriate interventions, based on theory Y assumptions, can unleash the inherent potential of the poorest performers in our organizations. As with many things in this book, however, it is useful to reflect on such theories with a healthy dose of scepticism.

Peter Drucker, for example, was far from convinced that theory X and theory Y assumptions, or any motivational theory for that matter, were of any real value to an organization, despite 50 years of intense research by psychologists.[29]

Still, we are sometimes left with people who perform poorly in our organizations and there comes a point when we need to ask some difficult questions. Firstly, is it worth the effort developing the skills, knowledge and capabilities of those who perform poorly in our schools? Should we really expend valuable energy trying one strategy after another in an attempt to improve performance? Should we really give up the time to micro-manage such individuals when we have other pressing issues to deal with? Is it fair to go through this process while other colleagues have to work that bit harder to compensate for the inadequacies of the poor performer? There is, indeed, a danger that you'll upset the highest performing people when you don't effectively deal with the worst.[30]

These difficult questions arise because a *great* organization, as opposed to a *good* organization, needs to have the right people 'on the bus', and the wrong people 'off the bus'. If we find that we've got the wrong person for the job, we should get them 'off the bus' even though it's an inconvenient, distressing and distasteful process for all involved.[31] Similarly, Drucker argues that senior leaders have a duty to remove underperforming individuals occupying key positions, for the sake of the organization as well as fellow employees: 'It may not be the employee's fault that they're underperforming, but even so, they have to be removed.'[32] However, there is a clear distinction between managing underperformance and guiding, teaching, coaching and mentoring people who are intrinsically motivated, disciplined and aligned, and importantly, getting results.

It would appear that an outstanding organization can only be created by the extraordinary performance of everyone, at every level.[33] But chances are, a third of the people you'll appoint in the future will not be suitable for the position, a third will be great in the job and the remainder will be somewhere in between.[34] You will therefore need to give some thought about how you will tackle underperformance. You see, as an aspiring leader, you will need to establish a worthwhile direction for the organization and do whatever is necessary to encourage people to move in that direction.[35]

And when you do have appropriate discipline and alignment, truly outstanding delivery will follow. Stephen Covey recounts a story about a hotel that was the venue for one of his training seminars. At first glance there was nothing special about this hotel, but it soon became clear that the staff were deeply committed to the wellbeing of the guests – nothing was too much trouble and outstanding levels of service had become the norm. Intrigued, Covey set about uncovering the secret that had led to such a commitment to service by all staff. And the secret was beautifully simple. The hotel manager had asked staff to contribute to a mission statement. And because everyone had the opportunity to contribute, all were committed to its realization: 'Uncompromising personalized service'. The message here is simply this; if you don't involve others in the process of defining the goals for either your niche project, department/faculty, or even the school as a whole, there will be no commitment to the mission.[36]

So when you involve others and recognize and appreciate their contribution, they are more likely to be motivated to overcome whatever obstacles they face. And while most people crave appreciation but say nothing, some people demand recognition for their contributions and achievements – a few examples to illustrate the point and make you smile: US President George Washington wanted to be addressed as 'His Mightiness', and Columbus pleaded for the title 'Admiral of the Ocean', and the great Victor Hugo wanted nothing less than to have Paris renamed after himself![37] (Incidentally, he got a street or two: Avenue Victor Hugo, Boulevard Victor Hugo.) Why not, therefore, reflect for a moment on the things you currently say in order to motivate and align your colleagues to the mission?

The Art of Public Speaking

OK, having now talked through the broad skills needed to interact successfully with other people and manage teams, let us briefly explore the art of public speaking. It is important to master this skill because it enables you to influence the attitudes and behaviour of others and will eventually allow you access to the upper echelons of your chosen career path.[38] We are going to take this opportunity, then, to refine our oratory capabilities.

It is probably fair to say that most people do not enjoy public speaking. It is also probably true that most of us only ever speak in public at weddings and funerals. It may be because it is such an unfamiliar experience that we dread doing it, but as you become more senior within school you will need to speak in public more often.

Once you know that you are going to deliver a presentation of some kind, you may start to feel somewhat anxious, even if the actual event is days or weeks away – this is known as an *anticipation reaction*, and it can last right up until the moment you take the floor. At the point you stand up and deliver the first few words you encounter an intense *confrontation reaction* which, thankfully, trails off after about a minute. From this point you begin to adapt to the experience and the degree of anxiety you experience returns to pre-presentation levels after about five minutes. The degree to which you're prone to these reactions is generally linked to your temperament – if you're a little neurotic you might find the experience a little more challenging than those who are more stable![39]

Of course, we need a little anxiety in life in order to perform well – it is just a case of learning to manage the tension so that it does not become debilitating. It is also worth noting that your audience will not necessarily know how nervous you are and, as with many things, the more you practise, and the better you prepare, the more comfortable you'll be come the moment of delivery. If, however, the thought of presenting to an audience fills you with terror, you might find it useful to think about your self-talk and what you can do to bring your feelings under control, as we discussed in Chapter 2. You may also recall that we discussed in that chapter a visualization technique. So next time you're faced with having to deliver to an audience try to see yourself in vivid detail – how does it feel to be stood before the audience when your delivery is of the very highest standards? Follow the process from beginning to end – hear your introduction and listen for the final applause. Internally rehearse the main content and ensure that every moment is top-drawer, second-to-none, simply flawless. That has got to be a good feeling, and it's a feeling you need to capture over and over again in the run up to the presentation.

Now, when you stand before an audience, you should bear in mind that your professional credibility with that group of people is on the line. So you have to work hard to win them over from the off. Your goal is to create a special bond, a magical rapport, that puts the audience at ease and establishes your authority. This sounds like a formidable challenge, but a confident start using a well-rehearsed opening statement, along with your general demeanour, goes some considerable way to making this happen.[40]

You might, of course, be tempted to write a script to read aloud to the audience – or, alternatively, you might memorize the script so you don't have to rely on reading it verbatim. Though you might be tempted to try this approach, don't do it! Instead, aim to speak extemporaneously – that means to prepare and practise what you're going to say, but allow the exact wording of each idea to occur as it is presented.[41] By speaking extemporaneously you will sound more credible and be better able to engage and sustain the attention of the audience. There is therefore a need to prepare an outline of your presentation – the sequence of key ideas and concepts that you plan to explore, but nothing further is required in terms of scripting. Once the outline of your presentation has been organized the secret is to practise, practise, practise until you can deliver your presentation extemporaneously within the given time constraints.

Of course, it's the delivery of extemporaneous speech that makes it so effective. And now, free from the tyranny of a script, you'll be able to concentrate on the delivery style. Let us, then, briefly discuss the infamous PowerPoint® presentation! There is a clear distinction to be made between 'death by PowerPoint®' and death by a poor presenter. Fascinating people, using extemporaneous speech, can deliver with the aid of PowerPoint® all day long without losing the audience. It is not therefore the fault of the technology if someone is boring you to death! Now, a sure-fire way to induce the MEGO effect (*Mine Eyes Glaze Over*)[42] is to read reams of text, or performance data, from projected slides. Your audience can read for themselves and don't therefore need you to repeat the content verbatim. No, concise bullet points and/or appropriate media (sound, image and video) are required which, handily, can also double-up as onscreen prompts for your extemporaneous speech. So, if you have yet to be subjected to this most appalling of experiences – death by a poor presenter, consider yourself lucky. If you have been guilty of inflicting the aforementioned pain, we'll forgive you, but only if you promise not to do it again!

So, as you're talking around the bullet points onscreen, how can you ensure that the delivery is engaging? Well, if you deliver your extemporaneous speech in a monotone voice, you're likely to lose the audience to MEGO before you get to the end of the first slide. The secret here is to develop a conversational style of delivery – that is, give the audience the impression that you're talking with them, not at them.[43] There are five elements to the conversational style of delivery to consider: enthusiasm, vocal expression, spontaneity, fluency and eye contact. As we know, enthusiasm is infectious and can therefore be used to grab the attention of the listeners. In terms of vocal expression, we've discussed the curse of the monotone voice, so let's now consider the antidote: variation in pitch, volume and rate of speech. It is important to punctuate the flow of words and change pitch and volume because such techniques can bring a real sense of meaning and drama to what is being said. One reason for not memorizing your speech is that it can sound somewhat stolid on delivery. The best presentations sound fresh and responsive as the speaker explores the prescribed themes – remember, the key is to 'learn the *ideas* of the speech – *don't memorize words*'.[44]

What you've read here might sound like basic common sense, but it is surprising how many apparently intelligent and capable people actually get this aspect of their professional life horribly wrong – you might even witness denial: 'I don't do that when I'm speaking', only to then observe said colleague commit the cardinal sins. You know, it takes a real sense of presence to genuinely hear yourself speaking in the heat of the moment. It also takes presence to assess feedback from the audience and adjust accordingly, while still speaking. But the expert public speakers do this adroitly and with aplomb. You may not have any political affinity with the UK Conservative party, but their current leader, David Cameron, is somewhat acclaimed for his extemporaneous speeches and conversational style of delivery – take a look at his 2007 Conference speech and you'll get the idea.[45]

The final thing to mention is a piece of advice from one Jerry Weissman, whose counsel we may well heed: '. . . my professional advice to you . . . is never to tell a joke in a presentation'.[46] This does not mean excluding amusing anecdotes, incidentally – just keep away from jokes. And why, you may wonder. Well, even if everyone in the room does find the joke funny, it will distract attention from the main point of your presentation. However, a joke during a presentation can lead to disastrous consequences – just ask Gerald Ratner, who famously joked during a speech about the quality of goods in the Ratners Group chain of jewellery stores. It was a joke that ultimately cost Gerald his job and almost brought about the collapse of the entire business. We might also consider the repercussions of the dinner party jokes told by Conservative MP Ann Winterton – the first cost her a senior job and the second joke, told on a different occasion, saw Ann temporarily suspended from the party. The moral of the story: don't tell jokes!

Public Perceptions – Brand Management

Both Gerald and Ann saw their professional reputations, which had taken years to cultivate, virtually dissolve overnight. Regardless, however, of the incidents that caused the damage, they did at least begin with a strong identity, a personal brand, if you will.

In our celebrity-obsessed society we can easily identify individuals who successfully cultivate their own brand. Entire marketing industries spring up around footballers, pop stars and those who are famous simply for being famous. Ultimately it is us, the consumer, that sustains their fame through the act of buying the products linked to their names. You might have strong feelings about the apparent vacuous nature of these marketing machines and their products, but it is important to recognize that you, as an individual, are your own brand. You have unique selling points – those special skills and aptitudes that others call upon at various times. You therefore have a market value, as typically measured by your position on a pay scale. So how do you manage your personal marketing, your public persona?

While reading around personal branding, I came across an article in a national newspaper concerning the work of a personal branding guru by the name of Louise Mowbray. Louise argues that a convincing personal brand has four distinct characteristics. Firstly, the brand has to be compelling. In other words, there needs to be clarity and substance around who you are, what you can do and your future goals. However, your personal brand, secondly, needs to be authentic – there's no value in trying to portray yourself as someone you're patently not. And, thirdly, the key to establishing your brand is consistency. If, for example, you portray yourself as being a bit creative and eccentric, yet suddenly turn up in a sharp business suit and a serious demeanour, you'll just cause confusion (unless you decide to stick with the new look, of course)! Finally, your brand needs to be 'known'. When some special skill of yours is needed within your organization, you need to ensure that you are known for meeting that particular need.

So, if you were to develop a 'brand statement', in order to summarize the organizational problems you can solve, what might it say? Consider my brand statement, as a starting point: 'A creative planner ready to take on a challenge'. So 'creative planning' is the thing that I am known for by management (or so I'd like to think!). And when an organizational plan is required, I might be asked to take a lead. It is, incidentally, only in hindsight that I have seen this branding phenomenon occur for me personally. In other words, it wasn't a deliberate or planned process. It would appear that personal brand development occurs whether we plan for it or not – others invariably make judgements about the kind of person we are based upon how we present and conduct ourselves. It would seem sensible therefore to manage the process to our best advantage. After all, you wouldn't think twice about managing your brand when going for a job interview. And the whole point of *brand control* is to ensure that public perceptions of your product or service are properly managed and therefore consistent.

How, then, might you brand and subsequently market your niche role, your department, or even your school? Within the wider corporate world, it is a continual source of wonder that even the most mundane product can become a strong brand and be marketed with great fanfare.[47] How many more ways can there be to extol the virtues of a medicated shampoo, a range of sofas, a personal loan or car insurance? The marketers manage it, though, and you'll notice that every product has a unique selling point that solves a problem – often it's a problem you didn't even know you had!

Now, those in academia who study such things as branding argue that research over the past few years has emphasized the need to establish a strong emotional connection between the brand and the consumer: 'Modern consumers no longer simply buy products and services, instead they buy the wonderful and emotional experiences around what is being sold.'[48] Let me give you an example. There is a particular ladies' shaving system that promises to 'unleash the goddess in you'. Now, ladies, shaving your legs is about removing unwanted hair – that's the function of the product, but that is not what the marketers are selling to you. They are selling an image that appeals to your inner aspirations, an image that pushes your deep emotional buttons. You can only realize this inner image, however, by using the product, and only this brand of shaving system has the power to make you feel this good about yourself! Not convinced? Okay, what about this tag line: 'I'm lovin' it!' You don't get much more of an emotional connection than 'love'! The line is trying to establish a personal, emotional, human, sustained link between the consumer and the brand. So the function and capability of the product itself is actually somewhat secondary when it comes to marketing, because it's the emotive message that ultimately counts![49]

How can you pitch to your customers and connect with them in a deeply profound and personal way? We're not talking about putting your school's vision statement on the front of the prospectus here. No, this approach is more profound. This is the message that you send to potential students and their parents, and it goes something like this: 'Join us [our school, department or niche project] and we will put your family at the centre of our academic and pastoral universe because we are passionate about helping your child reach their full potential.' You'll notice that the emphasis is on the aspirational and emotional, and not the functional, aspects of your service. True, parents need to know that your school can 'deliver the goods', but your marketing appeals to their inner aspirations in order to capture hearts and minds.

But this emotional connection shouldn't just serve to attract students and parents/carers to your services. Could a well-executed and professional marketing strategy (from advert, to applicant pack, to interview day) help secure the best candidates for posts available in your school? Could local businesses be persuaded to enrich your curriculum through collaboration because of your marketing strategy? But remember the golden rule – make an emotional appeal surrounding the engagement with the brand, rather than detail the specific function. If, for example, you were showing a prospective student and his family around your department you would emphasize the benefits of taking your subjects: 'Ceramics students tend to leave here and take Fine Arts degrees or set up their own galleries and businesses . . .' You would not, then, detail the mechanics of your department: 'We have two Ceramics teachers, whom I'm sure you'll get on with. You will get three lessons of Ceramics on Tuesday. All coursework components are externally assessed . . .' and so on. That's not, according to the research at least, the best way to market yourself. Always, always, appeal to people's aspirations. Now, consider, how you might use this approach to show a prospective candidate around your department. Will you run through the detail of his potential timetable and talk about homework or uniform policy? Or will you talk about the great team ethos, the excellent professional development opportunities and the difference he can make to the lives of the students? You get the idea.

Returning, then, to your personal brand. Does this brand identity trigger a deep emotional, positive reaction among those with whom you work and serve? This emotional reaction isn't designed to get people buying material goods, but is designed to elicit trust and confidence so that people begin to share a common vision and align their actions to the greater good.

The Rise and Fall of Empires

Your marketing and branding activities are basically concerned with securing alignment and stimulating growth. The issue of growth is incredibly important if you face challenging circumstances such as declining student numbers or relatively low standards of attainment. Growth also matters if you're trying to expand your niche role into something more substantial.

Now, when you think about some of the biggest companies on earth, you can't help but be impressed by their ability to sustain their growth. It's hard to believe that Google, for example, was run from a garage as recently as 1998. Ten years, and a growth explosion later, it is a global brand worth billions.[50] Okay, so there aren't many schools which run their own businesses, and there aren't many aiming to become global, corporate giants. But it begs the question, is there a fundamental limit to how much improvement in performance can be made? Common sense would suggest that a company, for example, can only sell so much stuff to customers before the market becomes saturated. There must be, then, a fundamental limit to how much profit can be made. And for schools, there must be a fundamental limit on how well students and staff can perform. Well, all organizations experience 'limits to growth', where balancing factors act to impede further improvements in performance.[51] The secret to securing continual improvement in performance is to find a way to circumvent these balancing factors.

So what can we do when we believe we've reached our limits? How do we proceed, for example, when we've hit the achievement and attainment ceilings that frustrate us? Once the easy and obvious things have been done to raise attainment, there are, contrary to what you might believe at this moment, other strategies to deploy in order to further boost performance. It is important to recognize that world-class standards will not come by throwing in the towel and saying 'we've got all we can out of them', or 'their low aspirations are preventing further improvement in standards'. It might be true that your current paradigm, and its related strategies and time-honoured approaches, have led you down this performance cul-de-sac, but this is by no means the end of the story.

Be sure to know, however, that the ability to move on from this position will separate the good leaders from the truly outstanding, because this is the performance intersection that most leaders can at least reach, but from which few can truly build. It is this cul-de-sac situation that leaves good leaders scratching their heads once, that is, they've exhausted all the standard and obvious solutions. They are out of answers because the only route forward appears to be 'do more of the same', or else 'retreat and try a different path'. And as we tend to be risk-averse, we choose to 'do more of the same' and that consequently gives rise to 'more of what we've got'! How frustrating is that? As Albert Einstein once said: 'Insanity is doing the same thing over and over again and expecting different results.'

It is here, then, that we also find the axis around which the principles of leadership and management revolve. For leadership is about 'doing the right things' and management is about 'doing things right', as Drucker pointed out. So, a world-class leader will find new strategies to take the organization out of the cul-de-sac, and a world-class manager will implement those breakthrough strategies to the highest quality standards. And you are aiming to build both leadership (doing things differently) and management (doing things better) capabilities concurrently[52] in order to translate your vision into concrete outcomes for children and the wider community. This is therefore an opportune moment to introduce you to something called a sigmoid curve. A sigmoid curve is basically an S-shaped curve which is usually plotted on a chart where the horizontal x-axis represents time and the vertical y-axis represents whatever performance standards you're measuring:

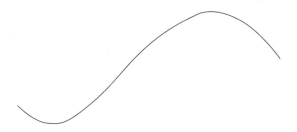

The relevance of this curve to the discussion may not be immediately obvious, but this curve illustrates both the predicament and points towards a potential solution to the thorny problem of growth barriers. That's a lot to ask of a simple curve! The curve basically illustrates the story of life, the rise and fall of empires, the progress of an epidemic,[53] student performance trends, profits growth, among other things. If, for example, you release a breeding pair of bunnies on a small island with no predators, the population will grow and decline as per the sigmoid curve. Once resources like food start to run out, the population peaks and begins to drop back as starvation kicks in – poor things. (You should know that no animals were harmed during the writing of this book!) Anyway, where we have had a run of continual improvement, we might overlay a sigmoid curve in order to predict what fate might have in store:

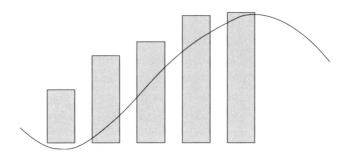

You can see how the sigmoid curve follows, approximately, the shape of the bars and it doesn't take a genius to predict what might happen if we continue operating as we have been doing. If you're looking at this chart and curve thinking 'but our GCSE/SATS performance is stable, in neither overall growth nor decline', here's a major revelation for you. You, and your organization, are preserving the 'steady state', and that is deeply problematic in this age of globalization and technological revolution, but more about that later.

So, many a company has seen their fortunes rise and fall in a similar sigmoid pattern. And when a business starts to detect the decline they try to find a new driver for growth – perhaps they develop a new product, or introduce a new marketing strategy. Perhaps they will fire half of the directors, but either way they look to do something to reinvigorate their sales and their profits – after, that is, they've tried the obvious solutions, like cutting costs by shedding excess staff. However, it is too late to start putting things right by that time because they are already on the back foot, so to speak, with declining sales/ profits. Wouldn't it be much better to devise new strategies for growth before the organization starts to go into decline? That's not rocket science, surely? You end up, then, connecting one sigmoid growth curve to another, as you can see in the diagram below:

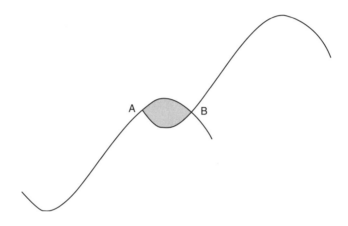

The point marked A indicates the beginning of a critical time for the organization because it may experience major upheaval as the new strategies begin to replace the old. If you follow the top curve on from point A it becomes clear that the organization actually takes a 'hit' in terms of performance – mostly because people are in a state of confusion and anxiety – making a change, remember, makes people feel uneasy as they're out of their comfort zone. What may not be immediately obvious from this diagram is that at point A on the original curve, there appear to be no issues to worry about because the performance trend is still on the up. Why, then, disrupt a perfectly functioning system? You'll have some explaining to do if you introduce new and innovative practice that only seems to disrupt performance and cause unnecessary confusion. In fact, the time spent between point A and point B would cause anyone anxiety because the changes you've implemented may not actually improve organizational performance in the long run – so you've taken a risk, disrupted routines, caused confusion and you may yet have got it horribly wrong! You might consider this period of time as the retreat back down the current cul-de-sac, as you go in search of another path, with the added pain of knowing that there's no guarantee of success at the end of it all. Who'd be a leader, eh?

Suddenly, though, growth in performance recovers and you'll notice that the new curve intersects the original curve at point B. The key observation here is obviously the direction of the two curves. The changes you've made have allowed you to break though the barriers that would otherwise have seen your organizational performance spiral downwards. Suddenly strong growth in performance returns and you can, for a while, congratulate yourself. But, of course, you know that you're going to have to go through the process again in order to realize the start of growth curve number three.

It is not, however, easy to move from one growth curve to the next – our mental models of the world lock us onto the existing curve and prevent 'next-curve' thinking.[54] So we must be prepared to abandon everything we currently do in order to survive in the future.[55] Of course, the organization's *purpose* and *values* remain, it is just the *method* that has to go. If we just pause for a moment and absorb those comments, we might shudder in horror – no wonder people don't much like change!

The challenge, then, is to '. . . ride the breaking wave of constant change even if you can't see the shore or the sky'. And if that isn't challenging enough, Bennis and Thomas remind us that history and precedent probably won't help to guide us on our journey.[56] In other words, past triumphs and well-worn strategies are not likely indicators of future success. Experience and courage gained along the way will, however, help to facilitate the jump to the next improvement curve. If you want to become an outstanding leader, you must be able to make, at the appropriate time, the strategic leap to the next growth curve in order to keep the organization moving forward.[57]

So, can you think of any companies that seem to rise and rise and rise, as in the diagram above? Can you think of any organizations that tend to yo-yo as they react to the decline and get a temporary 'bounce' from an intense 'more of the same' response – only to fall back again because it's impossible to sustain the 'same curve' pressure in the face of decline? Perhaps the organizations that continually grow have learnt to intercept the sigmoid curve before growth peaks and understand that continual innovation will keep it fresh and competitive. If you were to investigate the culture of this kind of company, what might you find? Might you find an organization that understands the nature of reality and keeps a laser sharp focus on its objectives? Might it be that this organization knows how to adapt and can quickly adjust to accommodate new process and systems? What, then, of the stuck business – perhaps they find themselves head scratching and panicked, when all of the obvious solutions have failed to deliver growth. How frustrating it must be for them!

Fascinating though this is, the message is hopefully clear. Look for new drivers of growth – those things that will enable your headline performance to improve year-on-year. It is critically important to make these changes before the external world forces change. Consider that within a visionary organization '. . . the drive to go further, to do better, to create new possibilities *needs no external justification'.*[58] There should be no need, for example, to wait for an internal crisis, or external pressure like Ofsted criticism, before doing the things necessary to affect change. The drive, as we've said before, needs to be intrinsic. But this does not make for a comfortable place to work. If you go out to build a visionary school there will be no room for complacency, no opportunity to put your feet up, or indulge in self-congratulation. You need to remain innately dissatisfied with current standards and current methods and, consequently, seek to venture out to explore new territory.[59]

Think Systems to Find Solutions

But it's just not that easy to break new ground. Actually, it sometimes feels like a battle to get even the simplest of jobs done. Why is it that the organization seems, on occasion, to be conspiring against you? How many times, for example, have you prepared a learning resource and found that you can't print it because the toner has run out and no one has thought to get it replaced? You get the cartridge replaced, print a copy only to find, typically, that the photocopier is being serviced and won't be available for hours. Never mind, you can ask your Teaching Assistant to copy a class set for you (if you're lucky enough to have a TA) but then remember that he's out on a course. Sound familiar? Now, it's not a case of simply being more organized – you are trying to reach an objective, e.g. photocopy some resources, and the school systems seem to be fighting you. You know these malfunctions are not deliberate, but you do sometimes wonder if someone has got it in for you! Well, according to Dr W. E. Deming, our quality expert, the workforce is only ever, at most, responsible for 15 per cent of the problems afflicting an organization. The remaining 85 per cent are the fault of systems. OK, this is a very simplistic view of organizational life, and I wouldn't take it to heart but, more often than not, it is the system that causes a crisis, not external forces and not an individual's mistake.[60]

One of the major revelations of senior leadership is that you, in your managerial and leadership capacity, hold responsibility for those systems. Consequently, it is within your power to evaluate the effectiveness of the systems and implement improvements. So, let us take a look at how this might be done.

Now, you don't need to become an expert in 'systems theory', but the basics will help alleviate some of the frustration you feel when you push to get something done only to have the organization push back. Basically, it goes like this. Your school, or any organization for that matter, is composed of a number of interrelated systems which are operated at some level by people, yes? Now, the difficulty with complex, interrelated, systems is that a failure in one part may have a cause that's some 'distance' away. When you can't easily link the cause to the effect, it can make putting things right very difficult and lead to immense frustration. You can't easily pin blame on, or quickly fix, system faults that you cannot readily trace, but the consequences of the failure are very real.[61]

The skills to learn, in preparation for senior leadership, are, firstly: to 'think systems' when faced with an organizational performance problem; and secondly: to 'zoom out' from a specific problem, like no toner in a printer, and try to grasp the wider scope of the system that encompasses the failure. Thirdly, consider where you fit within that wider system and ask if you are inadvertently contributing to the problem. At first glance, you may think: 'no problem, I'm independent of the system and not therefore at fault'. But it's a little more complex than that, and you need to reflect carefully before discounting yourself out as part of the cause. So, look to the system components and identify your own role. Draw flow diagrams to map the interrelationships between processes. Work through the diagram with your teams, discuss the system, gather data, agree the protocols and make adjustments as necessary. This is a very practical approach to help ensure that any improvement priorities arising from self-evaluation are translated into coherent, planned action. But you have to make a conscious decision to map, shape, streamline and simplify the systems. As Edward de Bono points out: 'Simplicity is not natural. You have to choose to make it happen.'[62]

So, you can choose to intervene to improve systems, or else ever have to tolerate their faults or compensate for their inadequacies. 'Shifting the burden', as Peter Senge describes it, is the principle whereby a failure in one process is 'fixed' by a another compensating process. It is the metaphorical 'papering over the cracks', rather than addressing the underlying problem, which typically arises because a proper fix is perceived to be too challenging to implement. In order to solve such fundamental issues, you have to make the effort to comprehend the systems in their entirety. Indeed, the ability to see the whole will bring new insights and help you to create the capacity to deliver the results you're looking for.[63] Make no mistake, however, you will need to make a fundamental shift in your perspective, and your thinking, if you're truly to bring the whole system within the scope of your conscious mind. But this is exactly what expert leaders learn to do. They perceive large-scale, meaningful patterns within their operational domains and respond effectively to well-structured, recurring problems or reflect, diagnose and ultimately solve those problems which are less structured.[64]

So, systems thinking can be used as an engine to power organizational change. After all, the modification, or implementation, of systems is the final and critical act to ensure that new ways of doing things are sustained.[65] And great systems lead to great organizational performance. In fact, the world's most successful businesses become great because of their underlying processes and organizational dynamics.[66] Make no mistake, 'People matter, but so do systems, rules and procedures.'[67]

That has been the briefest of summaries of what is, in fact, an incredibly fascinating subject. And because systems thinking is a potential tool to help you drive up standards, you might want to read a book called *The Fifth Discipline* by Peter M. Senge. This text is often cited and well regarded by academics and practitioners alike. I have to say that Senge's book served as something of a starting gun for my own leadership and management journey. And much of what I read I was able to apply directly to my own personal and professional circumstances. In fact, much of what is discussed in this book – mental models, personal mastery and systems thinking – is inspired by Senge. It is highly readable, so why not make this the very next leadership and management book you read?

The Key Concept

Hopefully, by this point in the book you will have started to think about your organization in very different terms. Now you see interweaving systems, a new reality, levers of power, a brand and an emerging business model. Perhaps you now see the organization as a dynamic entity shimmering in the haze of perpetual ambiguity. Perhaps you now have a deep sense of the whole and will be comfortable dealing with complex issues that cannot, or will not, fully resolve upon demand. Once you are in that psychological space you can hope to make the genuine transition from the operational to the strategic side of the organization. The ability to 'make like you're the boss' means that the concepts covered in this chapter become part of your everyday thinking about the way your organization functions.

We are therefore ready to revisit from Chapter 1 a fundamental leadership and management principle. Ultimately your core purpose as leader is to 'preserve the core *and* stimulate progress'.[68] The core consists of your organization's fundamental purpose and values. Progress – through *evolution* or *revolution* – is, well, the glittering path to world-class standards. As a school leader you must stimulate progress through a combination of challenge and high levels of managerial support.[69] If you are to be successful you must therefore have a very clear understanding of your guiding principles and core values. You must have a clear vision of your personal and professional future – how will your niche role, department/faculty, or school look and feel once significant progress has been made.

And if you find that your performance trends are not fundamentally tracing out a sigmoid curve, you are not stimulating progress. You are instead working to preserve the steady state – so what are you going to do about it? How can you harness the collective skills and abilities of your colleagues in order to secure progress? How can you win the hearts and minds of your students and their families in order to help those young people realize their potential? How can you become more effective without simply resorting to working longer and harder?

You may not immediately have the answers, but you know the situation is problematic – it is simply unacceptable to preserve the steady state. Will breakthrough innovation stimulate progress? Will a fundamental rethink find a route out from the cul-de-sac? As both leader and manager, can you make the transition from good to great?

With those questions in mind, let's now proceed to the final chapter.

6 | Oh Yes, Don't Forget About the Children!

'Every generation needs a new revolution.'

Thomas Jefferson

How odd, you might think, that a book about school leadership has barely mentioned young people in any direct or substantial manner. Yet the pursuit of world-class standards of provision for both children, and the wider community, has been the core mission throughout. By shifting the emphasis away from the individual child to the quality of the overall process, we can see the intersection between learning and teaching and leadership and management. We see, then, a robust approach for improving the educational outcomes for young people which is concerned with, first and foremost, improving organizational effectiveness. So, the needs of young people and the wider community have never been far from my mind.

It is, of course, important that children develop as well-rounded individuals; that they are happy and feel safe at school – outcomes which are not easily measured, but valued nevertheless. Of course, no amount of happiness or 'roundedness' will compensate for a lack of qualifications where a desired career path is concerned. But a happy and 'rounded' child is more likely to be an achieving child. Those children who cannot find happiness, and who perhaps cannot work in a team, or get themselves organized, or work independently, present particular challenges, as we shall see later. So, schools need to deliver, in partnership with others, a happy, safe, well-rounded, conscientious, entrepreneurial, achieving, qualified child to society. No pressure then!

We have been concerned with securing your contribution to these outcomes for students across an entire organization, and not just those young people you come into contact with on a day-to-day basis. In order to be highly effective, I've argued that we have to adopt various leadership and management practices and go through a process of personal mastery. Now, you might be something of a diehard cynic when it comes to the whole self-help phenomenon, but much of this ideology is not the claptrap you might take it to be, according to psychologist Martin Seligman at least.[1] At this point in your career you will, of course, have already secured your primary role, whether as a qualified teacher, finance manager, premises manager, and so on – but your mission from this point forward is to develop new capabilities in order to drive up standards across the sector.

You see, the warm words you'll sometimes hear from some quarters, about caring for children as individuals, are seldom accompanied by the ruthless and relentless pursuit of higher standards. Now, you might feel that the narrative in this book has sometimes been a little cold. You may indeed feel that the heart and soul traditionally associated with the learning and teaching process have been threatened. However, these two dimensions of schooling – moral purpose and effective delivery – are not mutually exclusive. For you, an aspiring senior leader, heart and soul can never again be enough on their own. With heart and soul must come strategy and execution. Charles Handy draws upon the eloquence of Christian symbolism to make the point: we need 'an outward and visible sign of an inward and spiritual grace'.[2] So moral purpose needs to be translated into high-quality provision, for every recipient of your service – students, parents/carers, wider community, and your colleagues. If we are to translate moral purpose into world-class provision, we have to break out of group-think mode, acknowledge our self-delusions, face the hard data, and commit to improving our practice/provision for every young person. And Drucker reminds us of the need to remain '. . . action focussed, rather than allured and overfascinated with introspection'.[3] So be passionate about learning and teaching, but be equally passionate about leadership and management. When that passion is translated into action, children will be even better equipped to face the challenges of the 21st century. And what challenges they face.

The Not So NEET

If there is one thing we know for certain, it is that education can transform your life; so with education and skills comes the hope of a brighter future. Yet some young people in our most disadvantaged communities are having none of it. They opt out, preferring instead a life of worklessness and, in some cases, a life of petty criminality, or worse. For example, a typical 'day in the life' of a 16-year-old male who is NEET (Not in Education, Employment or Training) appears to consist, at least in part, of being '. . . out with the boys on the estate. Chilling – terrorising, tipping stuff off bridges.' In the run-up to becoming NEET, school experiences consist of, for some: 'Fighting with people, and me getting expelled . . . I gave abuse [to staff] all the time.'[4]

For some young people, schooling clearly isn't meeting their needs. Indeed, for many young people school neither engages nor equips them.[5] This is all the more problematic if school happens to be the only place where a young person can escape the chaos of personal circumstances. What if school is the only place where behavioural 'norms' are articulated and enforced? What happens if school does not meet a young person's needs and there is nothing, and no one else, to show the way? We may perhaps watch those disaffected and disenfranchised young people then age and become parents themselves. They will inevitably perpetuate the cycle of low aspirations, poor skills and economic disadvantage among their own children.[6] It paints a depressing picture, and few would argue about the moral imperative of breaking this repeating cycle of wasted human potential.

So, if we really listen to children, and consider the economic challenges facing both the country and individuals, we have to revisit the moral purpose and perhaps challenge the assumptions upon which current practice is based. However, the sheer diversity of modern-day society means that no one has the moral authority to decide what education should look like for everyone.[7] The traditional view of education might embody such concepts as a 'conversation between the generations of mankind', or an introduction to 'the best that has been thought and said'.[8] It is, perhaps, the rejection of such concepts, and the lack of alternatives, that now sees a quarter of a million young people, or thereabouts, languishing in the NEET category.

And then there is the other end of the achievement spectrum to consider. Those students who apparently thrive in the school system but are unable to sustain progress in the wider world. As Anne Jones, a headteacher, noted twenty odd years ago, perhaps the basic assumptions on which schools have been operating are no longer appropriate: academic achievement, individual success and the route to employment are but one side of an educational coin. On the flip slide is co-operation, caring and coping.[9] It is therefore with interest to hear Charles Handy argue, after some considerable time reflecting upon his own journey through life, that: 'Learning is *not* finding out what other people know, but is the process of solving our own problems.'[10] Inter-generational dialogue and philosophizing perhaps need to be replaced with the development of emotional intelligence competencies and the adoption of problem-solving strategies.

If so, it begs the question: why do we insist upon transmitting knowledge between generations, when most of the knowledge needed by young people is, or could be, available online? Why not, instead, just teach the capability required to access and apply that knowledge on an 'as needed' basis? After all, 'the great aim of education is not knowledge but action'.[11] I acknowledge the significance of uttering such educational heresy, but can our society afford not to do it? Can we otherwise sustain the economy upon which we all fundamentally depend?

So why not therefore restructure the entire curriculum, and its delivery system, around capability? Ironically, the knowledge economy doesn't actually require, first and foremost, knowledge from its workforce. But a knowledge-based economy does require communication skills, reliability, punctuality, perseverance, teamwork, critical thinking skills, responsibility for self and others, independence, creativity and enterprise.[12] Teach those capabilities as a core curriculum instead! Such a change would represent a very long walk, by a very brave leader, back down the education cul-de-sac.

Futures Thinking

Now, CERI, the educational research arm of the Organization for Economic Co-operation and Development (OECD) has done some futures thinking and envisages six scenarios for the future of education:[13]

◆ In Scenario 1 – Bureaucratic Systems: '. . . schools are anchored in powerful bureaucratic systems. Strong pressure for uniformity and the fear of change combine to make the schools resist fundamental transformation, despite criticism of the school system by the public and the media'.

The question is, for Scenario 1, how long can the education system resist calls for change in the face of changing economic circumstances and obvious social inequalities?

◆ Scenario 2 – Focused Learning Organizations, sees schools become revitalized through diversity, innovation and experimentation, although still fundamentally concerned with knowledge transfer and academic competence.

◆ Scenario 3 – Core Social Centres, envisages schooling of young people to be the responsibility of the wider community – from businesses, religious groups, to higher education institutions. In essence, we begin to see the decentralization of the learning process, with students learning in a variety of settings, resulting in 'substantial blurring in the lines of demarcation between schooling and the broader environment'.

◆ Scenario 4 is the Extended Market Model, where schools '. . . become just one component in the diversity of educational systems, alongside privatisation and public/private partnerships'.

◆ Scenario 5 – Learning in Networks, would see conventional school disappear altogether, instead replaced by home learning or small community learning groups supported by a learning professional. Online communities could bind interest groups together both locally and internationally, all supported by sophisticated ICT.

◆ The final Scenario, number 6, is that of a System Meltdown precipitated by a teacher shortage. The shortage might be triggered by an ageing society, competition for graduates from other sectors of the economy, or declining belief in the education system.

Reading through these scenarios, it appears that much of the education system is traditionally anchored in Scenario 1, with Scenario 2 coming a close second, thanks to the Building

Schools for the Future (BSF) and academies agendas. I therefore offer you a question, or two, to contemplate: Are current educational reforms radical enough to keep pace with socio-economic demands, given that inter-generational knowledge transfer and academic competence is still the core mission? Are we in danger of getting the same old practice in brand-new packaging? Is there a chance that current reforms will better meet the needs of those young people who are interested in a 'conversation between the generations of mankind', or an introduction to 'the best that has been thought and said', while leaving everyone else marginalized? Either way: 'We cannot continue to give rhetoric to the skills, attitudes and knowledge that young people need for the 21st century while we, leading and teaching in schools, continue at best to offer shallow, indeed, cursory change.'[14]

Perhaps we need to embrace more fully Drucker's concept of breakthrough innovation throughout the entire sector and therefore create a new type of educational enterprise focused on the development of a different set of core knowledge competencies.[15] Surely we need a clean break from current conventions because incremental, iterative change is not appropriate for the globalized world in which we now live: '. . . strategic choices must be made not just to reform but to reinvent education systems so that the youth of today can meet the challenges of tomorrow'.[16] After all, 'every generation needs a revolution', as Jefferson provocatively asserts.

Actually, we need to go beyond a shift in attitudes and behaviour if we are to realize a quantum leap in performance – we need to change our view of the world, our view of people and our view of leadership and management practice. In other words, we need to develop a new reality,[17] a cultural revolution, no less. Our organizations therefore need to build the capacity to affect nothing less than a paradigm shift.[18]

And perhaps we are beginning to see a paradigm shift in the entire system. We have discussion about the roles and responsibilities of schools, a willingness to try new things, discontent with the current situation and debate over the fundamentals – all classic symptoms of transition to new practice.[19] Of course, this doesn't mean much hasn't been achieved in recent years, but it has hardly been a revolution. When speaking about paradigm shifts in science, incidentally, a famous physicist named Max Planck remarked that new scientific realities don't win converts on the strength of the evidence, but eventually win over because the old opponents eventually die off.[20] Yes, indeed, even in the face of overwhelming evidence, some people will still deny the obvious shortcomings of their current reality. There are undoubtedly people working within the education sector who hold very traditional views about the role of education in our society and who are either unable or unwilling to accept substantive change. We might therefore expect those people to defend their beliefs all the way to the grave, regardless of how many socially disenfranchised people, such as the NEETs, are sitting metaphorically beneath their nose.

I make the point because if we see the same pattern of paradigm shift in science repeated in the education sector (and it is a big 'if'), we might expect another century, or more, to pass before we see a transformation away from 19th-century delivery practices. It is, of course, sobering to contemplate the countless number of young people who may, during that timeframe, find themselves living with the unpleasant consequences of unrealized potential. It is, perhaps, a little strong to suggest that 'much educational change is akin to rearranging the deck chairs on the *Titanic*',[21] but fundamental reform is arguably required.

Can You Contribute?

Can you, then, the senior leader of tomorrow, contribute to a paradigm shift in education? Can you begin to use some of the tools and strategies identified in this book to transform your school, or are you inclined to perpetuate what has gone before? Can you overcome the choking bureaucracy that epitomizes the delivery of today in order to shape the systems of tomorrow? It can at times feel like an overwhelming challenge, but it is worth remembering that successful school leaders draw on the same basic repertoire of leadership practices: building vision, developing people, redesigning the organization, managing teaching and learning.[22] That's it, nothing more is fundamentally required of an effective school leader. The leadership and management principles outlined in this book will help you to develop just such a repertoire because the principles transcend both time and the specific function of any organization, whether it be educationally focused or otherwise. There is no reason to believe that the education sector has any genuinely unique leadership and management problems to solve – they are but variations on a theme.

Although you might be inclined to adopt some of these tools and strategies more readily than others, it is important to realize that you need to embrace an element of all. There is little point, for example, in crafting an inspirational vision if you cannot translate the ethereal into concrete action and results. Similarly, there is limited value in becoming emotionally attuned to your colleagues if you do not also adopt rigorous reality testing and systems thinking. It's all part of the leadership and management continuum: self-control through to organizational discipline, core values and beliefs through to a relentless drive for continual improvement. An outstanding organization has the capacity to embrace it all, indeed an organization can only become truly outstanding if it embraces all.

And in the final assessment, it comes down to you because nothing matters as much as the behaviour exhibited by the leaders.[23] The frightening truth, as Collins and Porras point out, '. . . is that *you* are probably as qualified as anybody else to help your organization become visionary'.[24] And there is your mission, as you pursue your senior leadership role: to contribute to the outstanding practice in your organization, day in and day out, until the quest for world-class standards becomes deeply ingrained into the fabric of your organization. And once you begin to get results, with your winning formula, adapt again in order to greet the next breaking wave of change. Continue to set new goals and seek new growth, in order to inoculate yourself against 'destination disease'.[25] Beware, therefore, the alluring glow of comfort and contentment, for therein lies mediocrity and stagnation.

Learn to live on the edge of your comfort zone, learn to identify the 'firsts', even the seemingly insignificant firsts: the first staff training session you deliver, your first meeting with an LA representative, your first presentation to the leadership team, and so on. If the 'firsts' start to dry up, ask yourself if you've become too comfortable and if therefore you need to seek a new challenge; if the learning stops, the problems start. As you climb to the top of one steep learning curve, go find yourself another to conquer, before you're prompted to do so by your line manager. Take control of your own professional development, learn to love learning and go seek out the 'firsts'. Simple.

The key message, then, is that you can't simply cherry-pick the fun aspects of the job if, that is, you want to be effective as a senior leader. There are significant challenges to overcome, and the ability to take responsibility, and tackle the difficult issues, differentiates leaders at different levels within the organization. Look, senior school leadership may not be rocket science, but if it were that easy everyone would be a senior leader. So the choice is yours, and know this: a refusal to grasp the nettle, to see things through to a satisfactory conclusion, will be the beginnings of the glass ceiling that will prevent further career progress. Surely you're not going to let a few unpleasant or unappealing tasks prevent you from reaching the senior team?

The Long and Winding Road

Let us also ask this: once you've achieved your goal of joining the senior leadership team, are you going to stay there for the rest of your career? Presumably you'll want to become a deputy headteacher, then a headteacher at some point in the future? And what will you want to do after that? Take on a bigger school? Take on an academy, or perhaps a federation of schools? A national advisory role, maybe? And if that's where your distant future lies, how many more nettles are waiting to be grasped?

This extraordinary process of professional development, fuelled by a determination to conquer increasingly challenging roles, will eventually take you to places you haven't currently contemplated or believe impossible to reach. Developing and deploying this adaptive capacity is, according to Bennis and Thomas, the single most critical factor common to highly distinguished leaders.[26]

If you fully embrace the process, if you truly open yourself to the possibilities, the effect on your life will be transformational – you will gain a new and profound insight into yourself and the world around you, and you will consequently find new ways to be effective in both your personal and professional life. You will feel the benefits of this process whether you're young or old, and regardless of your current standing – that is, whether relatively junior or relatively senior in the organization. And despite the scepticism of Drucker and others, the positive change in your character will be real and will be permanent. You will move beyond a reaction-based existence, in which your response to events is dictated solely by the external forces buffeting from all sides. Instead you will chart a course, stay true to your values, overcome hurdles and avoid distractions. With new insights will come new meanings. Intuition and gut reaction will be augmented with purposeful action underpinned by rational thought. And because of this mastery process, and only this process, can you hope to see beyond the obvious and the immediate, to glimpse solutions to the toughest problems, to get beyond the mental models and the historical programming that impedes 'next-curve' thinking. So the point of offering controversial arguments isn't to irritate, but simply to illustrate that alternatives exist if you're prepared to disengage the defences and be truly open-minded. So feel free to reject my educational philosophy, and the associated values, but preserve the theory within which they are embedded because therein lies the kernel of transformational leadership.

So, the process is extraordinary; but it is a venture you must undertake alone. Ultimately, this is your journey. And while others may support and encourage, it is you who must face the challenge – leadership is at times a lonely business. Your amazing future is, however, there for the taking, if you can learn to embrace the process, and love doing the things that make others recoil in horror. And yes, it is daunting to know that you are on the front line. The politicians can provide much of what we need in terms of resources, legislation and the broad principles, but it is you, and your colleagues, that have to deliver an outstanding service. The truth is, if you can't 'deliver the goods' on this one, there's no one else to do it. It really is down to you.

Should you be frightened by the responsibility that you're placing upon your shoulders? A little, perhaps. But take comfort from the knowledge that you're not alone in shouldering the burden. We each tread our own lonesome route to personal mastery and senior leadership, but once there, we discover other intrepid explorers that have undertaken a similar journey. Such intrapreneurs are out there in education land, just waiting to meet up with you to share ideas. Your very last leadership and management task is, therefore, to find those kindred spirits. Share that world-class practice and cultivate a sense of connectedness with your like-minded peers.

So, this stage of your senior leadership journey has come to an end, but it is just the end of the beginning – you are forever a work in progress. You now have your 'map', and a selection of 'tools' to choose from, but the rest is down to you. Good luck, and whatever you do, don't forget about the children.

Notes

Chapter 1 – What's It All About?

1. SSAT (2006) *Essential Questions for Future Schools*. SSAT, pp. 6–7.
2. Ibid, p. 18.
3. PricewaterhouseCoopers (2007) *Independent Study into School Leadership: Main Report*. PwC, p. viii.
4. Bennis, W.G. & Thomas, R.J. (2007) *Leading for a Lifetime*. Harvard Business School Press. I've adapted the integrity tripod concept from p. 145 to better fit the narrative in this book.
5. Ibid, p. 81.
6. Collins, J. (2001) *Good to Great*. Collins, p. 1740.
7. Rosenzweig, P. (2007) *The Halo Effect*. Free Press, p. 156.
8. Drucker, P.F. (2006) *The Effective Executive*. Collins, p. xxiii.
9. Leithwood, K. & Day, C. *et al.* (2006a) *Successful School Leadership: What it is and how it Influences Pupil Learning*. NCSL, p. 67.
10. Senge, P.M. (1990) *The Fifth Discipline*. Century Business, p. 142.
11. DfES (2007) *Participation in Education, Training and Employment by 16–18 Year Olds in England: 2005 and 2006*. DfES. This source is a Statistical First Release: SFR22/2007.
12. LSC (2007) *Delivering World Class Skills in a Demand Led System*, p. 5.

13. BSA (2007) *Army Basic Skills Provision: Whole Organisation Approach – Lessons Learnt*. BSA, p. 6.
14. NCSL (2006) *Recruiting Headteachers and Senior Leaders: An Overview of Research Findings*. NCSL, p. 35.
15. See Leitch, S. (2006) *Prosperity for all in the Global Economy – World Class Skills*.
16. See Every Child Matters – Change for Children: http://www.everychildmatters.gov.uk/
17. See Governor Net: http://www.governornet.co.uk/
18. See Fast Track Teaching Programme: http://www.ncsl.org.uk/programmes/fasttrack/
19. Bennis, W.G. & Thomas, R.J. (2007) *Leading for a Lifetime*. Harvard Business School Press, p. 19.
20. Gardner, H. (2006) *Five Minds for the Future*. Harvard Business School Press, p. 66.
21. Senge (1990), p. 19.
22. See ATL, DfES *et al.* (2003) *Raising Standards and Tackling Workload: A National Agreement*.
23. PwC (2007).
24. Covey, S.R. (1992) *Principle-Centred Leadership*. Simon & Schuster, p. 173.
25. Bennis, W.G. & Townsend, R. (2005) *Reinventing Leadership*. Collins, p. 38.

Chapter 2 – Find Your Niche

1. Senge (1990).
2. Senge, P.M. & Scharmer, C.O., *et al.* (2005) *Presence*. Nicolas Brealey, p. 11.
3. Bennis, W.G. & Thomas, R.J. (2007) *Leading for a Lifetime*. Harvard Business School Press, p. 106.
4. Covey, S.R. (1989) *The 7 Habits of Highly Effective People*. Simon & Schuster, See Habit 2, p. 95.
5. Senge (1990), p. 156.

6. Leithwood & Day *et al.* (2006a), p. 77.

7. Bennis & Thomas (2007), p. 93.

8. Seligman, M.E.P. (2007) *What You Can Change . . . and What You Can't.* Nicolas Brealey, p. 95.

9. Bennis, W.G. (1989) cited in NCSL (2003) *Growing Tomorrow's Leaders: The Challenge.* NCSL, p. 38.

10. Robertson, J. & Murrihy, L. (2006) *Developing the Person in the Professional.* NCSL, p. 5.

11. See Senge & Scharmer *et al.* (2005), p. 122 and Senge (1990), p. 175.

12. Helmstetter, S. (1982) *What to Say When You Talk to Yourself.* Pocket Books, p. 70.

13. Gardner, H. (2006) *Five Minds for the Future.* Harvard Business School Press, p. 24.

14. See http://psychclassics.yorku.ca/Maslow/motivation.htm

15. Covey (1989), p. 135.

16. Flaherty, J.E. (1999) *Peter Drucker: Shaping the Managerial Mind.* Jossey-Bass, pp. 258–9.

17. Covey (1989), p. 134.

18. Seligman, M.E.P. (2006) *Learned Optimism: How to Change Your Mind and Your Life.* Vintage, p. 15.

19. Helmstetter (1982), p. 197.

20. Ibid, pp. 160–70.

21. Ibid, p. 204.

22. Ibid, p. 31.

23. Collins, J. & Porras, J.I. (2005) *Built to Last: Successful Habits of Visionary Companies.* Random House, p. 100.

24. Flaherty (1999), p. 253.

25. Drucker, P.F. (2006) *The Effective Executive.* Collins, p. 52.

26. NCSL (2003) *Growing Tomorrow's Leaders: The Challenge.* NCSL, p. 15.

27. Davies, B. & Davies, B.J. *et al.* (2006) *Success and Sustainability: Developing the Strategically-focussed School,* p. 61.

28. Collins (2001), pp. 1–16.

29. Handy, C. (1990) *Inside Organizations*. Penguin, p. 184.
30. Collins & Porras (2005), p. xvii.
31. Flaherty (1999), p. 221.
32. Ibid, p. 273.
33. Covey (1989).
34. Senge (1990), p. 142.
35. Bennis & Thomas (2007), p. 122.
36. Covey (1992), p. 253.
37. Senge (1990), p. 345.
38. Luntz, F. (2007) *Words That Work*. Hyperion, p. 83.
39. Collins & Porras (2005), p. 32.
40. Flaherty (1999), p. 272.
41. Bennis, W. & Nanus, B. (2007) *Leaders: Strategies for Taking Charge*. Collins.
42. Flaherty (1999), p. 163.
43. SSAT (2006). SSAT, pp. 11–12.
44. Collins (2001), p. 30.
45. Collins & Porras (2005), p. 77.
46. Handy (1990), p. 120.
47. Bennis & Thomas (2007), p. 10.
48. Crawford, M. & Kydd, L. *et al.* (1997) *Leadership and teams in educational management*. Open University Press, p. 66.
49. Walsh, K. (n.d.) *Leading and managing the future school – developing organisational and management structure in secondary schools*. NCSL, p. 2.
50. Drucker (2006), pp. 68–9.

Chapter 3 – Tell It Like It Is!

1. Bennis, W.G. & Townsend, R. (2005) *Reinventing Leadership*. Collins, p. 16.
2. Senge (1990), p. 155.
3. Flaherty (1999), p. 274.
4. Covey (1992), p. 187.

5. Creswell, J.W. (2003) *Research Design: Qualitative, Quantitative, and Mixed Method Approaches.* Sage, pp. 6–12.
6. de Bono, E. (2004) *How to Have a Beautiful Mind.* Vermilion, p. 140.
7. Creswell (2003), pp. 8–9.
8. Gill, J. & Johnson, P. (1997) *Research for Managers.* Paul Chapman, p. 23.
9. Strauss, A. & Corbin, J. (1998) *Basics of Qualitative Research.* Sage, p. 11.
10. Creswell, J.W. (1998) *Qualitative Inquiry and Research Design.* Sage, p. 202.
11. DfES (2004) *A New Relationship with Schools: Improving Performance through Self-Evaluation.* DfES, p. 4.
12. Ibid, p. 19.
13. Ibid, p. 5.
14. Peters, T. & Waterman, R.H. (1995) *In Search of Excellence.* HarperCollins Business, p. 7.
15. Bennis & Thomas (2007), p. xii.
16. Bennett, N. & Woods, P. (2007) 'Understandings of Middle Leadership in Secondary Schools: A Review of Empirical Research'. *School Leadership and Management* 27 (5), p. 458.
17. Handy (1990), p. 131.
18. The Arbinger Institute (2006) *Leadership and Self-Deception: Getting Out of the Box.* Penguin, p. 16.
19. Goleman, D. & Boyatzis, R. *et al.* (2004) *Primal Leadership.* Harvard Business School Press, pp. 92–4.
20. Collins (2001).
21. Covey (1992), p. 258.
22. Walton, M. (1986) *The Deming Management Method.* Pedigree, p. 67.
23. Hallinger, P. & Sindvongs, K. (2005) *Adding Value to School Leadership and Management.* NCSL, p. 15.
24. As it happens, I'm no statistician and need all the help I can get! I tend to turn to the ubiquitous Microsoft Excel software

package, but the more adventurous might have a go at an application called SPSS, a demo of which can be downloaded from the SPSS website. SPSS is not for the faint-hearted, but it is incredibly powerful at analysing and presenting data, once you know what you're doing with it. There are numerous books to help with using SPSS and interpreting statistics, but I personally find *Discovering Statistics Using SPSS*, by Andy Field, really user-friendly. But again, it's not for the faint of heart – don't expect to be producing comprehensive statistical reports within the hour!

25. Gill, J. & Johnson, P. (1997) *Research for Managers*. Paul Chapman, p. 23.
26. Leithwood & Day *et al.* (2006a), pp. 69–71.
27. de Bono, E. (1998) *Simplicity*. Penguin, p. 41.
28. Senge (1990), p. 22.
29. Walton (1986), p. 32.

Chapter 4 – Deliver the Goods

1. Flaherty (1999), p. 263.
2. Goleman & Boyatzis *et al.* (2004). See Appendix B, p. 253.
3. Seligman (2006), p. 101.
4. Davies & Davies *et al.* (2006), p. 66.
5. Flaherty (1999), p. 184.
6. Leithwood, K. & Day, C., *et al.* (2006b) *Seven Strong Claims about Successful School Leadership*. NCSL, p. 6.
7. Helmstetter (1982), p. 163.
8. Collins (2001). See the Flywheel Concept, p. 175.
9. Drucker (2006), p. 100.
10. Covey (1989), pp. 150–6.
11. Ibid, pp. 146–54.
12. I've merged the basic time management matrix presented by Covey (1989) on p. 151 with a few 'tips' offered by the

Business Balls Website: http://www.businessballs.com/timemanagement.htm

13. Covey (1989), pp. 153–4.
14. Leithwood & Day *et al.* (2006a), p. 11.
15. de Bono (1998), p. 140–2.
16. Flaherty (1999), p. 164.
17. John Donne (*Devotions*), in case you're wondering!
18. Hallinger & Sindvongs (2005), p. 23.
19. Capezio, P. & Morehouse, D. (1995) *Taking the Mystery Out of TQM*. Career Press, p. 2.
20. Covey (1992), pp. 251–2.
21. West-Burnham, J. (1992) *Managing Quality in Schools: A TQM Approach*. Longman.
22. Hallinger & Sindvongs (2005), p. 24.
23. Covey (1992), p. 253.
24. Walton (1986), p. 132.
25. Ibid, p. 60.
26. Hallinger & Sindvongs (2005), p. 17.
27. SSAT (2006), p. 18.
28. Handy (1990), p. 187.
29. Collins & Porras (2005), p. xii.
30. Ibid, p. 29.
31. Ibid, p. 88.
32. Davies & Davies *et al.* (2006), p. 34. It did make me smile!
33. Covey (1989) See Habit 2, p. 149.
34. Davies & Davies *et al.* (2006), pp. 35–6.
35. Covey (1992), p. 167.
36. Drucker (2006), p. xii.
37. Covey (1989), pp. 148–9.
38. PricewaterhouseCoopers (2007), p. vii.
39. Collins & Porras (2005), p. 140.
40. Hallinger & Sindvongs (2005), p. 9.
41. Ibid, p. 19.
42. Walton (1986), pp. 86–7.

43. Maxwell, J.C. (2003) *The 17 Indisputable Laws of Teamwork Workbook.* Thomas Nelson, p. 138.
44. Hallinger & Sindvongs (2005), p. 25.
45. Davies & Davies *et al.* (2006), p. 76.
46. Collins & Porras (2005), p. 147.
47. See Bennis & Thomas (2007).
48. Ibid, p. 117.
49. Ibid, p. 102.
50. Hallinger & Sindvongs (2005), p. 12.
51. Goleman & Boyatzis *et al.* (2004), p. 221.

Chapter 5 – Make Like You're the Boss

1. Covey (1989), See Habit 2, p. 109.
2. Handy (1990), p. 116.
3. Ibid, p. 117.
4. Ibid, p. 120.
5. Ibid, p. 119.
6. Covey (1992), p. 102.
7. Leithwood & Day *et al.* (2006a), p. 91.
8. Goleman & Boyatzis *et al.* (2004), p. 23.
9. Carnegie, D. (1981) *How to Win Friends and Influence People.* Vermilion, p. 175.
10. Ibid, p. 175.
11. de Bono (2004), pp. 89–106.
12. Maxwell (2003), p. 8.
13. Ibid, p. 7.
14. Ibid, p. 8.
15. The Arbinger Institute (2006), pp. 81–90.
16. Covey (1992), p. 108.
17. Carnegie (1981), p. 22.
18. PricewaterhouseCoopers (2007), p. vi.
19. Leithwood & Day *et al.* (2006a), p. 46.
20. Senge (1990), p. 146.

21. Leithwood & Day *et al.* (2006a), pp. 63–4.

22. Covey (1992), p. 192.

23. Ibid, p. 195.

24. Carnegie (1981), pp. 32–7.

25. Covey (1989), p. 235.

26. NCSL (2003), p. 6.

27. Handy, C. (1993) *Understanding Organizations.* Penguin, p. 36.

28. Leithwood & Day *et al.* (2006b), p. 6.

29. Flaherty (1999), p. 260.

30. Maxwell (2003), p. 60.

31. Collins (2001), p. 56.

32. Drucker (2006), p. xvii.

33. Peters & Waterman (1995), p. xxii.

34. Drucker (2006), p. xvi.

35. Leithwood & Day *et al.* (2006), p. 11.

36. Covey (1989), pp. 139–43.

37. Carnegie (1981), pp. 43–4.

38. Verderber, R.F. & Verderber, K.S. (2003) *The Challenge of Effective Speaking.* Holly J. Allen, p. 4.

39. Verderber & Verderber (2003), pp. 19–21.

40. Ibid, p. 138.

41. Ibid, p. 199.

42. Weissman, J. (2006) *Presenting to Win.* Pearson Education, p. 5.

43. Verderber & Verderber (2003), p. 204.

44. Weissman (2006), p. 205.

45. I last accessed this page in May 2008: http://www.conservatives.com/tile.do?def=conference.2007.video.page

46. Weissman (2006), p. 88.

47. I'm not implying here that your niche role, department or even your school is mundane! I am implying that a strong brand identity can be established for any product or service, including your niche role, department or school.

48. Morrison, S. & Crane, F.G. (2007) 'Building the Service Brand by Creating and Managing an Emotional Brand Experience'. *Journal of Brand Management* 14, p. 410.
49. Luntz, F. (2007) *Words That Work*. Hyperion, p. 18.
50. Take a brief look at Google's history: http://www.google.com/corporate/history.html
51. Senge (1990), pp. 95–100.
52. Davies & Davies *et al.* (2006), p. 37.
53. Handy, C. (1994) *The Empty Raincoat*. Arrow, p. 50.
54. Ibid, p. 60.
55. The idea that we must abandon everything we currently do to survive in the future is attributed to Peter F. Drucker.
56. Bennis & Thomas (2007), pp. 83–4.
57. Davies & Davies *et al.* (2006), p. 37.
58. Collins & Porras (2005), p. 84.
59. Gardner (2006), p. 83.
60. Senge (1990), p. 40.
61. Ibid, p. 63.
62. de Bono (1998), p. 44.
63. Senge & Scharmer *et al.* (2005), p. 45.
64. Leithwood & Day *et al.* (2006a), pp. 69–71.
65. Goleman & Boyatzis *et al.* (2004), p. 201.
66. Collins & Porras (2005), p. 41.
67. Goleman & Boyatzis *et al.* (2004), p. 222.
68. Collins & Porras (2005), p. 89.
69. DfES (2006) *2020 Vision: Report of the Teaching and Learning in 2020 Review Group*. DfES, p. 30.

Chapter 6 – Oh Yes, Don't Forget About the Children!

1. Seligman, M.E.P. (2006) *Learned Optimism: How to Change Your Mind and Your Life*. Vintage, p. 88.
2. Handy (1990), p. 134.

3. Flaherty (1999), p. 259.
4. The Nuffield Review of 14–19 Education & Training (2008) Briefing Paper 2: *The Life Circumstances of Young People*, pp. 6–10.
5. DfES (2006), p. 7.
6. See Leitch (2006), p. 22.
7. The Nuffield Review of 14–19 Education & Training (2008) Issues Paper 6: *Aims and Values*, p. 3.
8. Ibid, p. 5.
9. Jones, A. (1987) *Leadership for Tomorrow's Schools*. Blackwell, p. 203.
10. Handy (1990), p. 199.
11. Carnegie (1981), p. 21.
12. DfES (2006), p. 10.
13. CERI (2006) *The Starter Pack (Draft): Futures Thinking in Action*. OECD, Part III.
14. SSAT (2006), p. 12.
15. Flaherty (1999), p. 164.
16. CERI (2006), Part I, 4.
17. Covey (1992), p. 173.
18. Walsh (n.d.), p. 4.
19. Kuhn, T.S. (1996). *The Structure of Scientific Revolutions*. University of Chicago Press, p. 91 – I've adapted the argument here from the notion of scientific research to generic practice.
20. Ibid, p. 151.
21. I came across this phrase as an anonymous quote.
22. PricewaterhouseCoopers (2007), p. viii.
23. Ibid.
24. Collins & Porras (2005), p. 217.
25. Maxwell (2003), pp. 124–5.
26. Bennis & Thomas (2007), p. 93.

Index